MW00472782

THE PATH
OF THE
WARRIOR-MYSTIC

"Busting all categories and conventions, Angel Millar creates a new code of masculine development by uniting contemporary needs with esoteric wisdom to reintroduce honor, purpose, accountability, ethics, and effort into a culture that has astoundingly degraded or forgotten these ideals. As steeped in magic, rite, and hidden history as he is in good sense, Angel delivers the book on positive manhood for which our culture has been yearning. Cynics will never forgive him."

MITCH HOROWITZ, PEN AWARD–WINNING AUTHOR
OF *OCCULT AMERICA* AND *THE MIRACLE CLUB*

"In his impressively researched book, Angel Millar takes us step by step on a journey to authenticity. Citing images and examples from myth, art, and religion, he shows us men how to grow into our highest expression as males of both strength and uncompromising insight."

WILL JOHNSON, AUTHOR OF
RUMI'S FOUR ESSENTIAL PRACTICES, BREATHING THROUGH THE WHOLE BODY, AND *EYES WIDE OPEN*

"Throughout the ages, and in most traditional civilizations, there exists a masculine ideal: that of the warrior-poet, or warrior-mystic, who has been initiated into both the worlds of action and contemplation—the harmony of pen and sword. However, during our age of chaos, masculinity as an ideal is no longer recognized but actively demonized by the forces of deconstruction and distraction, and hence, many modern men are lost in a wasteland devoid of meaning, balance, and higher ideals. Angel Millar has taken upon himself the noble task of helping to restore this lost balance, and his book offers both traditional wisdom and sage practical advice specific to our time on how to re-embrace the heroic, perennial masculine ideal."

AKI CEDERBERG, AUTHOR OF
JOURNEYS IN THE KALI YUGA

"A comprehensive and intelligently written book on a topic of vital importance: the development of psychologically and spiritually healthy men living in the complex age of the early twenty-first century."

P. T. MISTLBERGER, AUTHOR OF
THE WAY OF THE CONSCIOUS WARRIOR

THE PATH
OF THE
WARRIOR-
MYSTIC

BEING A MAN IN AN
AGE OF CHAOS

Angel Millar

Inner Traditions

Rochester, Vermont

Inner Traditions
One Park Street
Rochester, Vermont 05767
www.InnerTraditions.com

Text stock is SFI certified

Copyright © 2021 by Angel Millar

All rights reserved. No part of this book may be reproduced or utilized in
any form or by any means, electronic or mechanical, including photocopying,
recording, or by any information storage and retrieval system, without permission
in writing from the publisher.

Cataloging-in-Publication Data for this title is available from the Library of Congress

ISBN 978-1-64411-267-0 (print)
ISBN 978-1-64411-268-7 (ebook)

Printed and bound in the United States by Lake Book Manufacturing, Inc.
The text stock is SFI certified. The Sustainable Forestry Initiative® program
promotes sustainable forest management.

10 9 8 7 6 5 4 3 2 1

Text design and layout by Debbie Glogover
This book was typeset in Garamond Premier Pro with Arquitecta and Warnock
used as display typefaces

To send correspondence to the author of this book, mail a first-class letter to the
author c/o Inner Traditions • Bear & Company, One Park Street, Rochester, VT
05767, and we will forward the communication, or contact the author directly at
www.angelmillar.com.

*For Kyler; for all our conversations on the Will,
art, and the higher individual.*

* * *

*My thanks go to Chris, my longtime friend
and closest companion in the Mysteries,
who kindly read the manuscript of this book
and gave me his thoughts, encouragement,
and suggestions.*

CONTENTS

INTRODUCTION

THIS BOOK IS A JOURNEY. And though the pathway lies before us all, only a few will see it, and only the braver souls will take it. Only those for whom this world is not enough. Only those who have begun to sense that there is something illusory about the way we live and have begun to feel uneasy about the propaganda that, though ever-changing, cannot be questioned. The pathway will be different for each of us. Perhaps for some it will lead to the mountains or into the forests, while for others it may lead into the busiest of cities. But for all of us, it leads within—away from comforting, disquieting, or addictive distractions and toward beliefs, ideas, practices, and the mental fortitude that sustained probably every culture and civilization prior to the modern world.

On this journey, you will begin to understand the ancient and classical conception of what we each can be: the warrior who cultivates mind, body, and spirit; the mystic with a vision for his life; or what the Confucians call Chun Tzu (the superior man or superior person). You will begin to discover who you are and what you can be. You will begin to glimpse your Higher Self.

Such a journey is an ancient one. It is that of Jason capturing the

1

Golden Fleece. It is the journey of the shaman who, in dreams, finds his soul being led to distant mountains and given the secret of healing.[1] It is the journey of the Zen Buddhist monk who goes to the city to see if it will conquer him or he will conquer it. And it is the journey of the artist, martial artist, author, inventor, and innovator who struggles against childhood illness, accident, or poverty to change the world.

Although we will look at different myths along the way, we will periodically return to the legend of *Sir Gawain and the Green Knight*. Written in England, probably during the late fourteenth century, it has some similarities to many other myths of cultures both East and West. To describe it very briefly, one Christmas, when King Arthur's court is feasting, the celebration is disturbed by the appearance of a mysterious green knight. The stranger enters the banquet hall and challenges a knight of the court to cut off his head, on the extraordinary condition that the knight will allow him to do the same to him a year later. The knights aren't keen to take up the strange bargain, but upon seeing their hesitation, Sir Gawain volunteers. The Green Knight hands over his ax and bends his head so that Gawain easily decapitates him. To his amazement, however, the Green Knight picks up his severed head and tells Gawain to seek him out at the Green Chapel in one year's time.

Though he must surely believe he will die at the hands of the Green Knight, Gawain soon leaves the comfort of the court and goes into the forests, where there is no shelter and where wild animals roam and bandits lurk. After almost a year in the wilds, Gawain comes across a castle, where he is given shelter but also finds his character tested. And finally, he arrives at the Green Chapel and faces the Green Knight—and his own mortality as well.

Increasingly, today, the newly born human being is regarded as a mere blank slate, and the role of education, it is believed, is to instill the "correct" information in the child so that he or she will grow to be a "productive" and nonthreatening member of society. But society itself constantly changes, believing one thing, then another that is contrary to the first. Yet the modern* human being must keep up. Consequently, for all his confidence and for all his technology and sophistication, the modern human being is essentially passive, constantly absorbing the latest beliefs and shedding the old ones, so that each person is able to continue to live in relative comfort, though never really knowing who he is or what he could be.

The classical understanding was different. The individual was fundamentally *not* a blank slate. He already had a soul. And that meant that he already had a "nature" or an inclination toward some things and away from others, even if, as a child, he was hardly aware of his own nature. Indeed, how many of us have stumbled across something in later life—a movie, a painting, a photograph, a novel, a martial art, a religious faith—that seemed to embody exactly who we were but had, yet, not become? Such an experience is emotional. Our heart jumps. We imagine ourselves—see ourselves—as a superior form of who we are now: more confident, more skilled, calmer, stronger, dressed differently, and living a different life.

We have mentioned the legend of *Sir Gawain and the Green Knight.* In another Arthurian legend, after the death of his father, Percival is taken to a forest by his mother and raised there. Although he is of noble blood, she fears that he might become a knight and keeps him ignorant of his nobility and of knighthood. But then, at fifteen years of age, Percival catches sight of some knights passing by and, sensing his destiny, immediately leaves his home and travels to King Arthur's court.

---

*I use the term *modern* to refer to the modern era, including "postmodernity."

There is much in this little tale. Percival's mother tries to shield her son from the world, to keep him from putting himself in danger. Yet once he catches a glimpse of who he could be, Percival leaves the shelter of his mother and seeks out his destiny, even though it is dangerous. Today, as if infused with the spirit of Percival's mother, Western society is increasingly preoccupied with trying to create a world that is safe—safe from confrontation; safe from ideas and opinions considered wrong, hurtful, or dangerous; safe from physical threat, accident, or viruses; and safe from risk itself. Doubtless, for many, a world in which the experts or the politicians tell us what we can and cannot do, say, or think in return for personal safety is a welcome trade. Yet for this we will have to sacrifice not only our freedom but also our spontaneity, self-reliance, risk taking, adventure, our will to push beyond our limits (or what we thought our limits were), and ultimately, our own nature. For the safety of a world that looks after us, we will have to sacrifice who we are and what we could become. And we will discover, too, that a life lived safely will leave us vulnerable to new and unimagined dangers.

1

The Dual Quality
of the Warrior

MAN IS A DIVIDED CREATURE. He compartmentalizes his life, thinking and behaving one way at home, another with friends, and another at work. The character he manifests is determined in part by the demands subtly, or not so subtly, placed on him. Coworkers, friends, and family members suggest what he should feel and how he should act. Even objects inform his decision and personality: a couch as opposed to an office chair, for example, or an ad for a vacation as opposed to one for a smartphone.

He moves through his day, beginning as one individual, then morphing into another, and then another. Some part of him is kept secret. His character at one time of the day is in conflict with it at some other time. He presents himself as a peaceful, saintly individual but fantasizes about revenge and violence against someone who crossed him, cheated him, or made him feel insignificant. He is a man of high ideals who thinks it permissible to swindle and cheat. He is a humanitarian who would think nothing of putting a bullet in the head of his neighbor if it benefited "humanity." He is a doting father and loving husband, but upon seeing a woman across from him on the subway for only a few seconds, he dreams of leaving everything behind, of starting a new life with her somewhere he has never been. He wants to rid himself of himself because he feels it—his "self," his life, his attempts to conform—to be an illusion. He is a contradiction that he has never attempted to resolve but only to disguise.

This contradiction lies deep in our bones. As zoologist Desmond Morris pointed out half a century ago in *The Naked Ape,* in his evolution, man went from a forest-dwelling, fruit-eating primate to a hunter and meat eater—a wolf with a more complex brain and an ability to make and use tools in the hunt.[1] And in this evolution, everything from his eating and sexual habits to his relationships had to adapt and change.

Yet in the contemporary era, through an emphasis on specialization—and on carving out a niche within a specialization—education and employment have encouraged our compartmentalization. We are not expected to know how the dots connect but only to focus on one dot—and to make it our life. We do not make the whole of anything, but only one part of something. The factory worker does not make a whole car, for example, but is employed in the area of the engine, the tires, or the paint. Nor does a garment worker sew together an entire pair of jeans, but is allocated only one part of the jeans (sewing on the same pockets endlessly, or sewing the sides, etc., but never the whole). Even at far higher levels of education and sophistication do we also find such disconnection.

We do not bridge different disciplines but endeavor to remain in our own. And we want to find the smallest niche within it so that we can be the "expert." When it comes to our identity and lifestyle, independent of our occupation, it is little different. We know to stick to one thing and to make sure we conform to one group, whether inherited or chosen. We are a registered Democrat or a registered Republican. (And we toe the party line.) We are a vegetarian or a vegan, or we are on the carnivore diet. And we are spiritual but not religious or religious—and political—but not particularly spiritual.

Yet the fundamental split in our culture is that of the intellect from the physical body; hence, our image of the intellectual man as physically weak and our image of the physically strong man as anti-intellectual, brutish, and primitive—"a knuckle dragger." Even this might have some basis in our physiology, for as Morris notes, man has both the largest brain and the largest penis of all primates, though we prefer only to acknowledge the former.[2] Yet while our evolution and even our physical body—with its oft-competing advanced brain and easily stimulated sexual organs—might play roles in our contradictory lives, the compartmentalization in our private and professional lives betrays a lack of a sense of oneness, practically and spiritually. We are not integrated beings.

There is a lack of curiosity and a lack of wonder at existence. In place of the mystical and in place of that sense of the profundity of being, we have fostered a siege morality—the weaponized morality of those who are "against." Every culture needs a code of morals, ethics, virtues, and values. But such a morality can't serve as a guide to elevate our actions and to integrate all aspects of our life. Rather, like conspiracy theory, religious fundamentalism, and popular occultism, it urges the individual to see everything through a simple formula that has been so arranged as to make disproving it impossible, even though it ultimately obscures the truth rather than illuminates it. But to those who have no real understanding of culture or who cannot create anything meaningful, it provides the perfect escape from engaging in a strange world and from having to look at one's own very real limitations in relation to it.

Nevertheless, siege morality has real-world consequences. It is used as a weapon against those whom the moralist disagrees with or feels threatened by and against those who act in accordance with their Will, since the moralist feels incapable of doing likewise. At its most pathological, siege morality becomes a kind of compulsive game, in which ever more microscopic faults are detected and the most innocent action or statement is held up as an example of heresy. But more than that, it locks the moralizer out of the realm of being. It always focuses him on others and *what they are doing.* It is as if the modern human being has imprisoned himself in a glass box of his own making. And he recognizes that only those outside the glass prison are truly capable of acting, capable of good and evil, capable of becoming themselves. Unable to bear the sight of it, he bangs on the walls, shouting and trying to get others to stop what they are doing. In a single, explosive moment, the walls are torn down and the glass is shattered.

In contrast, in classical societies, both East and West, the arts and sciences were seen as making up a whole. The educated gentleman had to know and to practice the arts of war and the arts of peace. Despite the brutality of battle, the higher type of warrior lived by an ethic. The weak were defended rather than exploited. He possessed a sense of the sacred and even an appreciation for the beautiful and the transient. In Japan, this type of warrior emerged as the samurai and in China as the *youxia.* Under Islam, such a warrior lived by the code of *futuwwa* ("young manhood"), and in medieval Europe, he lived by the comparable code of chivalry. Yet, even before this, in the Volsunga Saga, written in Iceland during the thirteenth century, though based on older legends,[3] the hero Sigurd is praised for being adept with the sword, spear, and other weapons, for learning "many courtesies"[4] or "good deeds"[5] as a young man, and for being wise.

Yet, claimed C. S. Lewis in 1940,[6] in the modern era, we live "among the ruins"* of the chivalric code. No longer associated solely with the medieval knight when Lewis was writing, the term *chivalrous*, in a practical sense, meant little more than politeness toward women. We can detect a similar transformation in our word *virtue*, which is derived from the Latin term *virtus*, meaning manliness, valor, bravery, strength, and so on. The *vir* in *virtus* means "man" or "a hero" and is related to the word *virile*.[7] But later, virtue, or to be virtuous, meant the opposite. It meant to be feminine, polite, to consider the feelings of others, and to keep oneself at an emotional and a physical distance. The virtuous were those who did not experience but remained somehow virginal to the world.

For Lewis, though, the essential and true quality of chivalry is that it places a "double demand" on the individual. It, in other words, acknowledges the dichotomy of man and requires the chivalrous to be fierce in battle but meek in situations of peace. In a sense, the chivalrous man is one of extremes, not merely being fierce now and polite and courteous then, but also being maximally fierce and yet detached, meek, gentle, or polite. But he is so only as appropriate. And in this sense, he is a man who is self-contained and self-controlled, a man of energy, ready for any situation and ready to give all of himself.

Our vague cultural memory of chivalry and this conception of the meekness of the knight mean that we tell ourselves that the brave man is always gentle and that the bully is always a coward. But Lewis denies

---

*In recent years, this phrase has become associated with Julius Evola, an author of works on spirituality, traditionalism, and politics, due to his book *Men among the Ruins* (Inner Traditions). No connection is implied.

this, pointing out that there are men who are courageous in battle who cannot easily find a place in society during peacetime and who might, perhaps, only find a home in an asylum for the criminally insane. The warrior is not the only type of individual who finds it difficult to fit into society, of course. As with an adult who claims to see spirits, a child who daydreams or who dreams too vividly, has too much energy, or has imaginary friends is no less likely to find himself at least heavily medicated during some period of his life, though in the ancient world, he might well have found himself initiated into the vocation of the shaman. The uncompromising and visionary artist is another figure who has often found adjusting to convention to be a challenge.

Men, in general, face a particular challenge today. Whether we like it or not, the capacity for violence has been associated with masculinity and has been prized in men by all premodern cultures, whether those cultures were European, Native American, African, Arabic, or Asian. The capacity for violence meant that a man could hunt and kill an animal for food and could, and would, if necessary, fight and defend his family, friends, tribe, or people. His capacity for violence gave him, as well as those he was bound to in some way, a better chance of remaining alive and free.

The man who was able to perform extraordinary acts of violence in service of his family, tribe, or people (or sometimes religion) was eulogized in myth and tales: the dragon slayer, the man who enters a ring of fire, the man who wins back the Golden Fleece, all with more than a splash of blood along the way. Such myths are still with us. They may be remodeled and are often given a modern or futuristic look for the movies or television, and the hero might be fighting for democracy, equality, or human rights, or fighting against inequality, sexism, or xenophobia, but the hero remains one who is capable of violence and who uses it.

We have not changed much over the last few hundred thousand years or more. Though we like to tell ourselves that we are civilized, loving, caring, and altruistic and believe all people are special, we nonetheless find ourselves attracted to the woman with childbearing hips; a small waist; and large breasts, eyes, and mouth, and to the man with physical strength, confidence, presence, and a capacity to eliminate any threat to our security.

Some men, of course, have found a solution to the problem of knowing how to be a man in modernity by turning purely to the intellect. Such men are often physically weak, soft, and nonthreatening in appearance but very knowledgeable about a range of obscure and specialist subjects. They might even reject "masculinity," ostensibly out of political conviction, though perhaps also with a twinge of fear. And although incapable of physical violence, such men will often be more than capable of intellectual violence, denouncing and degrading those whom they regard as the political enemy or those whom they recognize as more physically impressive and more sexually attractive to the opposite sex.

Lewis pointed out this essential quality of the modern West, which we have already touched on: the intellect and body have been separated, with those who privilege the intellect disdaining the body—especially physical strength or physical beauty—and those who privilege the body looking down on the soft and intelligent. There is a fairly well-known saying—often wrongly attributed to Thucydides—from Sir William Francis Butler's biography of Charles George Gordon. He says, "The nation that will insist upon drawing a broad line of demarcation between the fighting man and the thinking man is liable to find its fighting done by fools and its thinking by cowards."[8]

Now that such a society has come into existence in many parts of the West and perhaps elsewhere, we can see what happens when a culture separates the body and the intellect—and, by extension, the warrior and the thinker.

We are aware of the brutality of war—the torture of captives, the raping of women, and the acts of violence by the soldier, who then cannot integrate back into civil society. But this has doubtlessly always occurred. For millennia, the taking of slaves, the ritualistic killing of civilians, and the rape of women were all seen as part of the spoils of war. The Norse were known to splay open a defeated enemy's chest, sacrificing him to the god Odin. But the Aztecs were far more imaginative. Their prisoners of war were considered to make the best sacrifices, and they were treated with great respect prior to being brutally killed. But at some point, they would be taken and their heart would be cut out while it was still beating. Then their corpses would have been ripped apart, cooked, and eaten.[9]

More novel is the man whose thinking need not be tested by physical reality or who feels he does not need to be capable of defending himself, or even willing to. With an almost willful lack of understanding of human nature, modern man insists that the government should be omnipresent and powerful enough to protect him, yet benign enough not to use that power against him, even when he himself stands against the government.

When mind and body have become split, culturally speaking, society begins to equate physical strength with moral weakness and beauty with ugliness. But how does a society arrive at this point? As Lewis warns in his essay on chivalry, societies go through cycles. Ibn Khaldun (1332–1406), the great historian of Arab culture, had observed this six centuries earlier. In his lifetime, he had watched as dynasties ascended, only to flourish for a short time and then collapse. According to Ibn

Khaldun (who appears to have influenced Lewis's essay on chivalry), the life of a dynasty would last only three generations or, we might say, would have three stages.[10]

In the first stage, a band of warriors would conquer an existing dynasty and would begin to rule it. This new elite was fierce. Its members remained loyal to each other and exalted physical prowess and glory. Hanging on to their harsh "desert values"—or what, in America, might be called "frontier values"—they cared nothing for luxury.

In the next stage, the following generation would adopt the trappings of civilization. They enjoyed luxury. But they also retained a respect for strength and glory and hoped that the old values would return.

In the final stage, however, the third generation would forget the desert values and would think only of luxury and safety. Unable to fight, those of this generation would demand protection from the ruler. But since his people no longer had the ability to defend themselves, the ruler would be forced to look outside to find and hire fighting men who could maintain the peace. Eventually, recognizing that the dynasty was weak and dependent on them, these fighting men—who lived by the old desert values—would swoop down and take over.

Although Ibn Khaldun was writing about Arabic and North African society, it is notable that we find a cultural sifting away of physical mastery elsewhere. In Greece, before the fifth century BCE, the notion of *aretē* (excellence) was associated with the courage and physical strength of the warrior. Afterward, despite the fact that they themselves were associated with both morally questionable behavior and the intentional use of fallacious reasoning to win any argument,[11] the Sophists began teaching young men in aretē, though they associated it with moral virtue. And of course, Lewis had pointed out something similar with the notion of chivalry.

A similar, cultural shift from the physical to the intellectual occurs through the work of one of the more influential philosophers of the last few centuries, Georg Hegel (1770–1831). Hegel, who had a significant influence on Karl Marx, came to believe that philosophy had advanced so far that it—or reason or dialectic—had surpassed theater, art, and music, rendering most of culture obsolete. "What is rational is real; And what is real is rational,"* declared Hegel.[12] The nonrational, it is implied, is unreal.

Part warrior, part philosopher, we must cultivate rational thinking. But we cannot withdraw from the world and into the intellect, neglecting the body. The real, after all, is mostly experienced in the nonrational: the physical body, our family, friendships, brotherhood, love, sex, a sense of exertion during physical training, a sense of wonder in looking out into the natural landscape, and so on. The essence and Mystery of life has been expressed, and deep meaning found, in poetry and literature, in the simple act of sharing a meal, in tradition and custom, in painting, in music, and in the arts more broadly. Though the intellect is necessary, mere intellectualism does not satisfy us deep down.

Since Hegel, there has emerged an industrial-type use of language for criticism that is unnatural to us. It has a conveyor belt–like—even hypnotic—quality to it. It is draining, soulless, and predictable. As the philosopher Ernst Cassirer observed, since the most ancient times, words have had both an everyday "semantic" function and a "magical" function. While the former type of word describes things, the same word can be used, magically, by the shaman to "produce effects and change the course of nature." But, says Cassirer, in modern propaganda, the same phenomenon has reappeared. There, we find not only

---

*Was vernünftig ist, das ist Wirklich; und was wirklich ist, das ist vernünftig.

the transvaluation of values but also the transformation of human language. Most particularly, we find that in propaganda—and, we could add, in criticism and cynicism—the "magic word takes precedence of the semantic word"[13] and is used against reason itself.

Yet the critic, the intellectual, is consumed by his own words. Japanese literary author Yukio Mishima (1925–1970) claimed that, in his own life, words had taken hold of his consciousness long before he had acquired a consciousness of the body. As an author, his understanding of language served him well. At twenty-four, his controversial novel *Confessions of a Mask* was enthusiastically received by the Japanese public, launching him to literary stardom in his home country. Soon, Mishima would become the best-known Japanese author in the West, and later, he would be considered for the Nobel Prize in literature. Nonetheless, for Mishima, words were "corrosive." They made reality abstract (for the purpose of communicating facts, ideas, and feelings), but this had the effect of eating away at reality itself—like ants feeding on a pillar of wood, Mishima would say.[14]

There is another type of spiritual corrosion that the sensitive male feels today. Plunged into a world without a tradition, one that demands neither that he become heroic nor that he surrender himself to the Divine but asks him merely to settle for a life of consumption, fitting in, and being the same as everyone else (while being told that he is special), the individual attacks himself. He criticizes himself. He knows, or feels, that his personality is a mere mask and that behind his niceness, his sociability, his placating smile, lies a dark and terrible desire to conquer or to be conquered, to push beyond all limits and pull back the curtain to see life in its absolute nakedness—its essence, cosmic patterns, and plan revealed to him—even if it, Medusa-like, might paralyze and destroy him.

But he has been born into a time in which men are tame, and he, as a man, must seek a respectable profession and must follow the rules. He must not, at all costs, probe his primal instincts and become a wild man, a man on the margins—an artist high on drugs and dreams, seducing his models, or a poet torn between sex and heroic death. In his criticism of himself, he takes on society's criticism of manhood, partly to reject its most barbarous aspects and partly to feel it—even as something wholly negative, something demonic—within himself. He wants to destroy himself so that he can search through the rubble and ash to find a small seed of gold. He wants to be thrown into an experience that might destroy him in order to discover who he really is.

For Mishima, as for us, split from each other, the mind or the body can plunge itself into its own world so that the individual becomes too intellectual or too physical, but not peaceful in himself.[15] Recognizing the problem, the Japanese author devoted himself to bodybuilding and kendo, acted in gangster movies, and starred in a photoshoot called *Barakei* (Ordeal by Roses) by Eikoh Hosoe, where he posed nearly naked. Mishima scandalized Japan, but like a dancer, he thought his ideas out through the body as well as through the written page, placing the mental and the physical on the same level and reuniting them with each other.[16]

Traditionally, the physical world was regarded as the world in which the spirit is manifest. Things themselves express a transcendent meaning. In the church, the scenes depicted in the stained glass windows, like the paintings of the illuminated manuscript, could be read by the illiterate. They told a story. Prior to the invention of the Gutenberg printing press, books were written out and painted by hand. The expense of producing a book meant that what was recorded had to be of value to the owner, not just for a few days but for a lifetime. And prior to the invention of writing, the myths, rituals, and morals of cultural and religious traditions were memorized. The brahmin, the village elder, the storyteller—all of these sustained society by recalling its tradition, which itself aimed to keep a careful balance between the world of men and the world of the gods.

Language was mystical and creative, and those skilled in it—the philosopher, the enchantress, the sorceress, the poet, the priest—were believed to occupy a place somewhere between the ordinary human and divinity. With their words, they could reveal the hidden yet essential truth of existence, appeal to the gods and goddesses for their favors, or reveal or shape the destiny of the individual or the tribe. Their words— their spells—could change the physical world itself, bringing rain or lightning, causing healing or sickness, or making someone fall in love or perhaps out of love. And they could read nature as if it were a book, predicting future events upon seeing a flight of birds or the appearance of an unusual animal.

Words, language, and, later, writing and even individual letters were regarded as partially otherworldly. The gods (e.g., the Egyptian god Thoth and the northern European god Odin) invented or discovered writing. According to Kabbalistic theory, God created existence through the use of the Hebrew alphabet. And in Christianity, the Word (*Logos*) of God was believed to have become flesh in the person of Christ. Far from being mere stories, the myths of the world's cultures described the process of Creation, the nature of existence, and the attitude and behavior of the heroic individual.

But uncreative and unable to take the same kind of risk as the creator, the modern critic always keeps himself at a distance from the physical. The theater critic has never put on a play. The music critic is not a musician. And the art critic cannot paint. We might think that this makes their opinions worthless, but at the foundation of such criticism is the assumption that the intellectual is able to view and to know more than the creator precisely because he does not sully himself with the dirty business of actually creating something. In academia, too, there is the belief that a scholar should write about things that he does not practice because this will ensure that his opinion is fair and unbiased. But a non-Christian writing about Christianity or a non-Muslim writing about Islam is as likely to be as biased as a Christian or a Muslim writing about his respective religion, though the bias might be different or opposite. And the same goes for probably every other subject.

When we talk of the intellectual and the critic, however, we are speaking not of a profession, per se, but of someone whose understanding and capacity have withdrawn to the intellect alone. While the critic is concerned with the lives of others, another type—the pessimist—is concerned with his own life and with the lives of those who he believes share his fate. A kind of inner, preemptive surrender, pessimism is a strange luxury, and it is indulged in either by those who believe that optimism, by tempting fate, will be proven wrong (and so, they secretly hope, might pessimism) or by those who wish to appear serious, hardened, and uncompromising in a world that strikes them as compromised. But pessimism is itself the ultimate compromise. Settling for fate rather than striving toward destiny, it is unheroic and anti-initiatic in spirit. And it must be discarded at the outset.

Similarly, though they often go together, we should not make the mistake of conflating the creative with the artistic. Someone painting landscapes in the French Impressionist style may well be highly artistic but merely imitating; he is not creative. Creativity is about solving problems, while criticism is about pointing them out or, if they do not exist, making some up. But more than that, creativity is also about seeing—and acting on—possibilities. And at its best, it gives us something new, aesthetically inspiring, and meaningful, expressing the perennial anew and awakening our own deep sense of purpose.

The shift in vision from the critical to the creative is a shift in consciousness from seeing oneself as the passive victim of circumstance, as someone who has things done to him, to seeing oneself as someone in control of his life and actions—as, in other words, someone who acts in the world. This shift can be extremely difficult, and some will resist no matter the cost. But such a shift in consciousness must be made and, perhaps, must be made several times in the course of a lifetime as one is assaulted by loss and periods of struggle.

To give up our sense of victimhood may seem an obvious step, but as the Armenian mystic and spiritual teacher G. I. Gurdjieff observed, a person will often give up pleasure, but he will not easily let go of "his suffering."[17] We see this most obviously in the religious devotee, ideologue, or critic who has renounced normal pleasures yet uses his belief system to justify his hatred of others, which festers over many years. Such an individual has come to see himself as—and finds his importance in being—a victim. In his own mind, he is a kind of cosmic or "heroic" victim. He alone has taken on suffering as a self-sacrifice. He alone is wounded by the vicissitudes of life. And naturally, he believes, he would be happier, more successful, and more fulfilled—all of his dreams coming miraculously true—if he had not been forced by fate (and by some particular group that can be blamed) into such a role.

But as composer Jean Sibelius once remarked, no statue was ever erected to a critic.[18] And if we are to move toward becoming the kind of man who is remembered for his heroic struggle toward the good—even in his own life—then our first task is to kill our inner cosmic victim. In premodern societies, this would have been done with the aid of the village elders in an act of ritual initiation. The boy, when he had reached the age of manhood, would have been put through some ordeal, some ritual of transformation or of a symbolic death and rebirth, or some test that would push him out of the realm of childhood.

We can enlist the help of others once we have reached the point where we know we must kill our inner victim. Though less common than ever, this might well mean being initiated into a brotherhood that offers community, healthy challenge, and guidance—formal or informal. And certainly, being part of a group is invaluable. But you must do the necessary work on yourself. And the first task is to refocus, aiming your mind and actions toward the good.

In *Body, Mind, and Spirit,* Elwood Worcester and Samuel McComb describe how a prominent "man of science" transformed his life by transforming his thinking. The unnamed scientist was "unhappy, ineffective and obscure." He had read about positive thinking but had dismissed it. Then he decided to put it to the test for one month. He stated,

> During this time, I resolved to impose definite restrictions on my thoughts. In thinking of the past, I would dwell only on its pleasing incidents. In thinking of the present, I would direct attention to its desirable elements. In thinking of the future, I would regard every worthy and possible ambition as within reach.

The scientist felt more content, his colleagues were soon more cooperative and helpful, and, more peculiar, having craved the recognition of certain eminent figures in his profession, the scientist suddenly got a letter from the "foremost of these," asking him to become his assistant.

Can we say for sure that there is no embellishment or exaggeration in his account? No. But the central claim that the "personality seemed to attract, whereas before it had repelled"[19] is to be expected in the shift from critic or cynic to creator, from cosmic victim to a man of energy, enthusiasm, and positive action. Moreover, such a shift in thinking is absolutely necessary for each of us.

Today, not only is society divided into those who are dominated by thinking and those by the physical, but it also is divided into factions of worldview, with those adhering to one worldview regarding themselves as the victims of the other, and vice versa. It is normal to identify with a group of some kind. With factionalism, however, people are almost permanently in a state of stress and feel under siege. Their overarching concern is to feel "safe" even as they attack others. Consequently, they defend, downplay, or ignore bad ideas and ignoble behavior when they come from their side and attack, condemn, mock, and even intentionally misinterpret good ideas—so that they can claim to be morally outraged—when they come from an opponent.

As you are concerned with laying the foundation for initiation, self-discovery, and the discovery of the sacred in your life, your identity must not be a matter of conforming to ideas or to the morality, theory, or ideology du jour (all of which were thought up by others and are parroted to the point of meaninglessness). You are not what other people say or do, no matter how much attention they may receive. You are not the latest social theory. You are not the ideology thought up decades or a century or so ago. Nor are you what you stand against. No, your identity must emerge out of your lifestyle. You must conceive of yourself as what you do and where it is likely to take you. And if you are unhappy with that, then you must begin to strive toward doing something different and better.

The Roman emperor and Stoic philosopher Marcus Aurelius said that a man should adhere to two rules in his life: first, to use reason as his guide, and second, to be ready to change his opinion.[20] Instead of identifying with a faction, you must identify yourself with quality—both of thought and of the character of the individual. This means that you will be critical of—or at least you will not identify with—reprehensible behavior just because you are on the same "side" as the perpetrator and that you will not knowingly perpetuate lies even though others might be and even though those lies might work to your advantage.

In associating yourself with quality, you will listen only to those who are intelligent and thoughtful, who display good character, and who attempt to understand and to speak the truth. Rather than dismissing others, you will test your ideas against theirs. However, precisely because you associate yourself with quality, you will not engage in arguing with the unintelligent and vulgar. Instead, embody your higher ideals—strength, dignity, composure, thoughtfulness—so that your superiority of character is evident.

Instead, you should seek out the opinions of the most intelligent representatives of views you disagree with and earnestly seek to understand their positions. Take, for example, the third Mughal emperor of India, Abu'l-Fath Jalal-ud-Din Muhammad Akbar. Though a practicing Muslim himself and a ruler who was not obligated to listen to anyone, Akbar opened religious dialogues with Hindus and Jains and was influenced by some of their customs and ideas. Like Akbar, your aim is not to find something to convert to. It is to learn, to understand, and to feed your mind and heart. In a sense, it is to know and to become more your real Self.

The terms *thesis, antithesis,* and *synthesis* are often used to describe the dialectic or thought of philosopher Georg Hegel, whom we mentioned earlier. Here, your perspective is the "thesis." The opposite point of view is its "antithesis." And the new perspective that emerges from the clash of the two is the "synthesis." However, this new perspective is also a new thesis, or a new starting point, and it, too, will be confronted and transcended. And so on, and so on, with your understanding of life continually expanded and refined.

However, your aim is not only to continually discover the synthesis of your convictions with other perspectives, which are embodied in different traditions or arts, but also to create a synthesis in different areas of your life and different aspects of your consciousness: fierceness with meekness, intellect and body, tradition and invention, the desert values or frontier values with an appreciation for culture, spirituality combined with an appreciation for the material world, and positive thinking with the ability to acknowledge and cope with challenges.

In our own time, it is especially important to cultivate a healthy relationship with the physical. Technology has not only amplified the voice of the critic (including our own inner critic), but over the last century, it also has increasingly reduced the role of the physical. We drive instead of walking, text instead of writing with a pen and paper, and call on the phone instead of meeting to talk in person. Moreover, increasingly, we do not feel the need to be part of a physical community and prefer to join "communities" online, even where the members are anonymous or semianonymous.

Although, in modernity, new technology has generally been introduced as laborsaving or as a new form of entertainment, such technology (car, smartphone, computer, etc.) invariably becomes obligatory for work and employment. Instead of using technology for pleasure, we must keep up with it to survive. And the more laborsaving devices we use, the less time, it seems, we have for anything.

We have already looked briefly at the mental importance of cultivating a positive attitude, creativity, and the ability to contemplate different ideas of quality. But it also is essential for you to return to and to cultivate the physical. First and foremost, this should mean training in some kind of physical discipline, such as a martial art, self-defense, or weight lifting, depending on your age and health. Check with your doctor to make sure you are healthy enough to begin a physical training regimen. If you genuinely are not, take up a gentler exercise such as tai chi or qigong. If you can, learn and practice an art such as painting or playing a musical instrument or learn something else that requires the use of your hands. Walking should become a part of your daily routine, and so should cooking. If you can't already, learn to cook and make your own meals each day or make cooking a part of your family activity.

Do not make yourself into a cliché. Defy easy categorization. Strive to cultivate what is uncomfortable to you. If you are a daydreamer and a romantic and consider yourself "soft," passive, intellectual, or artistic, cultivate skills of action, such as martial arts or an intense, physical sport. If you consider yourself to be "hard" or a man of action, take up meditation, write poetry, or take up painting. Learn from a master. Cultivate the different aspects of your being to become more three-dimensional, more fully present, more alive, and more difficult to classify. Cultivate a deeper and wider sense of your own being.

Take control of your life. Make things. Develop your body. Respect the great martial artists and the great poets. When men have nothing that they are passionate about, nothing concrete that they love and find engaging, nothing they can mold with their own hands and through their own sweat, they become fanatics about ideas, ideologies, and theories, which, although filling them with a sense of purpose, slowly drain the life out of them.

2

NOBLE FRIENDSHIP

IN THE TALE *SIR GAWAIN AND THE GREEN KNIGHT*, we come across King Arthur, the knights of the Round Table, and the ladies of the court celebrating Christmas. This is a time of religiosity, festivity, ritual, family, and friendship. All is going well. Spirits are high. There has been jousting, and now there is dancing and song. Then, in the midst of the festivities, a strange and mysterious knight enters. And everything changes.

The knight is tall and firesome looking. It is almost as if he were a giant. But there is something far stranger. He is green from head to foot, and he has come on a green horse. He does not wear armor like other knights. In one hand, he holds a sprig of holly and in the other a giant ax. The court falls silent, wondering who he is and what his intentions might be. He assures Arthur that the branch he carries signifies his peaceful intentions, and he points out that he is not dressed for battle. Instead of fighting, the Green Knight suggests a game. He will give any of the knights his ax, and he will stand there, unmoving, while the knight takes a swing at him to see if he can behead him (which would surely be inevitable). In return, exactly one year later, whoever takes up the offer will submit to the Green Knight in the same manner. [1]

As the philosopher Alasdair MacIntyre has suggested, the honor-based society can be compared to the game of chess. Courage is not separate from friendship. But rather, societal norms demand certain actions and obligations, depending on the relationship of one person to another. If a man is killed, either his kin or his friend must avenge the murdered by killing the murderer. Then, in turn, the friend of the original murderer must avenge his death, and so on, and so on. To fulfill one's obligations leads one inexorably toward one's fate and death, and the more friends and family members one has, the greater the risk of becoming embroiled in a vicious cycle in which the individual himself will be slaughtered.[2]

The honor of the knights of the Round Table has been challenged. Sir Gawain approaches the stranger and, after promising to do as agreed, takes the ax. The Green Knight stands still and bends his head a little, ready to take the blow. Sir Gawain raises the ax high, then strikes, easily lopping off the head of the stranger.[3] It rolls along the floor and is kicked, indignantly, by some of the other knights. Yet the body of the Green Knight does not lifelessly collapse. Instead, his body leaps forward, grabs the decapitated head, and storms off with it to his horse. Turning back to the hall, the Green Knight lifts his head high and tells Gawain to seek him out one year from now at the Green Chapel.[4]

Today, we are unsure what—if anything—constitutes male values or qualities. We have no sense of *virtus*, but only of virtues. Perhaps not even that. We noted earlier that chivalry and the attempt to create a superior type of warrior or knight can be found in many if not all developed cultures, from the Chinese and Japanese to the Christian and the Islamic—the latter with its notion of futuwwa (young manhood). Some of the qualities, characteristics, and skills of these warriors might be seen as more feminine today. The famed samurai Miyamoto Musashi, for example, was known for his calligraphy, painting, and landscape gardening as well as for his skill and ruthlessness in battle. But as uncomfortable as we may be with them in our own time, in the small sketch of the Green Knight and the knights of the Round Table, we find those qualities that traditional and classical cultures across the globe have regarded as essentially or primarily male: physical strength, the ability to engage in physical combat, courage, risk, a sense of honor, and a sense of the importance of keeping one's word.

We are more atomized than at the time when the Arthurian romances were written. And atomization encourages us to think that we do not need to work on the ordinary, even, perhaps, on keeping our word or what we might call our integrity. If we are learning an art or a martial art, we feel that we can skip the basic lessons and move straight to advanced practice. If we are an artist, we believe that, regardless of the quality—or lack of quality—of what we create, we will be able to sell our art with the claim that we have suffered or the suggestion that we are intellectually beyond the grasp of the ordinary person (i.e., that we are some sort of genius). And like politics, spirituality appeals to many who do not want to do the unpleasant work of facing who they are and getting their own lives in order. But that work is the foundation of all progress in one's life, spiritual or material.

The ordinary is the realm of beauty and ugliness, strength and weakness, of friendship and loneliness, love and loss, and it is there that we must battle our demons and must take control of our thoughts, emotions, and actions. Hence, though ending with the state of residing in God, in his description of the one hundred "fields" or spiritual states of Sufism, Abdullah Ansari of Herat begins the spiritual journey with repentance, magnanimity, and contrition. He ends with the sublime but begins with the ordinary. And that is where we, too, must begin.

It is in the ordinary that the cultured man is able to find and experience the mystical. Hence, eating a communal meal is important in many religious and spiritual traditions. And it is unsurprising that it should play such an important role in setting the scene in *Sir Gawain and the Green Knight*. The early Christians met communally to partake of the "love feast," or *agape*. The ancient Greeks held a *symposium* (literally, "with drink") after a meal, often for purely social reasons but also to discuss philosophy—hence, Plato's dialogue *Symposium* and Xenophon's work of the same name. Spartan boys and men ate a communal meal (*syssitia*), regarding it as a substitute for their family. Muslims meet together during Ramadan to enjoy the *iftar* ("break fast") meal together. And Masonic lodges also hold a communal meal at each meeting; a more ritualized and elaborate form of the meal is known as the Table Lodge.

Just as MacIntyre pointed out in regard to the obligation of one friend to another, an invisible architecture of rules, etiquette, and obligations characterizes and structures the traditional society, including those religious and initiatic societies that exist today. Overt displays of rebellion were unnecessary because even a slight departure from established etiquette would have signaled a dissenting attitude. Hence, anyone below the samurai in social status who did not bow to the warrior or who did not bow low enough was risking his or her head, which could be cut off on the spot without repercussion. The slight gesture of not bowing properly signaled infinitely greater dissent than the popular rants filled with expletives that we so frequently hear today but forget in an instant.

But the meaning found in such inflexible rules within a traditional society is not the punishment but the ability to communicate in a manner far more subtle—and to communicate far more deeply—than we find possible, in general, in the contemporary West. To cite a more positive example, in the Japanese tea ceremony (*chadō*), for example, the host turns the cup so that the most beautiful part is shown to the guest, and after receiving it, the guest rotates the cup so that the most beautiful area faces the host. In this way, each signals that the other's pleasure is more important than his own. It is a subtle gesture, but it says it all.

To exist even briefly in such a world is to experience something that might be called "psychic." One senses the feelings and thoughts of others around or through the ritual actions. But ultimately, the architecture of rules and etiquette points toward what is beyond the participants: to Fate, to destiny, to the Mystery of life, to death and what continues after it (one's soul and one's family, lineage, society, and so on), and to God or to the Tao. Hence, chadō is the *dō,* or the Tao or the "Way" of tea, just as kendo is the Tao or the "Way" of the sword. And as the late samurai manual written in the early 1700s, the *Hagakure,* tells us, one who practices a Way should understand it even more so when he hears of other, perhaps very different, practices of the Way.

Indeed, a culture manifests a certain conviction in different ways, even if it cannot articulate it in words. Look at the ink paintings of Chinese-educated children and the drawings of Western-educated children and you will notice in the pencil of the latter the same back and forth motion of the knife at dinner and notice the singular, swooping motion of the chopsticks in the brush of the former. This may seem insignificant, but in the motion of the brush, the painter exhales, becoming one with the brush and with the moment, experiencing and embodying the dō, or the Tao, while in the West, we have attempted to know the Divine through the technical—in cutting up or dissecting and examining the parts. (We will explore this in chapter nine.)

A basic assumption underlies everything, and one who rebels

against that all-pervasive assumption will often abandon many of the basic norms of society. He might, for example, eat food that does not require a knife and fork but that can be eaten with the hands. Or he might become vegetarian or, conversely, eat a diet that is mostly meat. He might take drugs, or he might entirely refrain from consuming alcohol. In countless ways, he signifies not only his dissent but also the philosophy or worldview to which he feels an allegiance.

Sharing food, eating together, and generosity are strongly emphasized in the Islamic futuwwa code,[5] just as they are in Christian chivalry. Why? Not only does this help strengthen the community, but it also inculcates an ethic, a way of being, in those who participate. In regard to the person who is receiving it, generosity is a lesson in humility. In regard to the person giving it, generosity can be regarded as the practice of fearlessness on a smaller scale. The individual gives what he has with the belief that he will be provided for himself, either through the reciprocal actions of those to whom he has given or by the Will of God. He does not have to worry about starving. (Even in the modern positive thinking movement, there is the belief that money freely given away, charitably, will be returned several times over in some other way.)

God and, consequently, ethical behavior also form part of the traditional communal meal, with, for example, a prayer of thanks to God for the food being offered before anything is eaten. If meat is to be consumed, then the sacrifice the animal made might also be remembered. The individual does not eat while half-focusing on work or on something else. The focus is on the Divine, the community, and the food that brings the physical more in line with the divine.

Excess in consumption or behavior is prohibited. The drinking of alcohol is prohibited (*haram*) in Islam. Drinking alcohol, tea, and coffee is prohibited in Mormonism. And the taking of intoxicants is prohibited in Buddhism. The medieval Icelandic text, the "Hávamál," advises us to drink in moderation. And likewise, Freemasons are instructed not to eat or drink to "intemperance or excess." No one is improved by drunkenness. Intoxication often leads to unwise things being said or done. Displays of gluttony or greed also reflect poorly on the character of the individual. In traditional societies, such as we have mentioned, the host eats last and insists on his guests eating whatever is left on the table.

The point of being a member of a group is not merely to have joined, of course, but also to contribute, to engage in mutual exchange, and to sharpen ourselves against the intellects and abilities of those who are with us. This implies accepting that we know less than those who are more advanced and having the humility to learn from them and—at least later on—being able and willing to advise those who are less experienced and who are seeking to advance in the group, whether it is of a spiritual, philosophical, or martial nature. This takes both confidence and humility: confidence that we know some things and have some ability or potential and the humility to accept that we have things to learn.

The atomization of modern society combined with cheap and immediately accessible entertainment via the radio, television, and, more recently, the internet has not only made it easy for the individual to avoid becoming part of a group that meets in the physical world but also to take pride in not being "a joiner." Yet in probably every society that has existed, East and West, an individual was part of something—a church or temple, a guild, an initiatic society, a fraternity, or a veterans' association. Our banding together with others goes back to the emergence of humankind. Without claws and teeth that could be easily used to kill and without thick, protective fur coats, the human being was at a major disadvantage to many other animals—from the bison to the lion and the eagle. It was our ancestors' ability to work together that enabled them to overcome their disadvantage and to be able to hunt and kill for food animals that were far stronger, faster, and naturally adept at using their bodies to fight and kill.

Close bonds enabled the survival of the clan or tribe. And important in any discussion of the spiritual, close bonds enable us know intuitively what someone is thinking or feeling, even when he claims the opposite. In extreme circumstances, a closely knit group approaching danger may well experience an almost psychic bond. Exile, then, was a punishment second only to execution and was often, in effect, a drawn-out death sentence. Even if the exiled individual survived somehow, he was forced into a kind of spiritual death, being cut off from the community and even from family and close friends and, we must add, from the spiritual body—the collective consciousness or the spirit or *egregore* of the tribe.

The root of our word *outlaw* is the Old Norse *útlagr*. This term referred to a criminal who, because of the severity of his crimes, existed outside the protection of the law. His property was destroyed or seized, and since the útlagr was legally a nonperson, he could be killed by anyone at will, and his killer could not legally be made to suffer any punishment or reproach. A less severe variation of exile is shunning, or the breaking of some or all relations between a community and an individual deemed to have broken its rules. Typically practiced by religious communities, shunning is still used by the Amish, Jehovah's Witnesses, and the Bahá'í. In theory, at least, it is intended to protect the community from outside influences (technology, alcohol, beliefs contrary to that of the community, etc.) that might threaten its cohesion and, ultimately, its existence.

What was considered the harshest of punishments in tribal societies and small close-knit societies, the modern individual chooses almost by default. Community has defined us as people, but we choose or are forced by circumstances not to have a community. If we live in a city, it is likely that we do not know our neighbors' names. We foster only superficial relationships with colleagues and even with many of our "friends," whom, deep down, we do not believe we can rely on in a crisis. Indeed, it is not unusual to keep from our friends our innermost feelings, fears, hopes, or plans. In all situations we are always somehow alone.

We could, of course, find a group to belong to—a close-knit band of brothers, a religious community, or perhaps even a martial arts school—but so hollowed out has the modern individual become that he might feel trepidation when he thinks of being closely bonded to others and the commitment that might entail. He might have to attend a regular meeting, giving up one or perhaps even as many as two nights a month. He might be duty bound to help a brother in need. Or he might feel pressured to give up some self-harming habit and improve himself, to bring himself in line with those with whom he now associates. There will be standards and expectations. It is much easier to watch television, to get drunk, to find "friends" online, or to practice some spiritual tradition alone, not learning from others and not being held accountable.

Even a century ago in the West, it was typical for men to belong to a fraternity and for women to belong to a sorority, for almost everyone to belong to some kind of social, charitable, or civic club. In the late 1970s, two-thirds of Americans still attended club meetings. However, from 1985 to 1994, there was a 45 percent drop in active participation in clubs.[6] The decline in participation in groups and societies is a new phenomenon. And such disconnection from a community has consequences: loneliness, anxiety, a rise in cortisol (the stress hormone), and possibly addiction.

Yet although it is unnatural for us, today an individual proudly announces his lack of involvement in and lack of commitment to any group. He is not a "joiner." He doesn't believe in "groupthink." Yet his clichéd excuses, his thinking, and his type of "individuality" are commonplace. He has friends and affiliations, of course. But in the types of groups we are considering—the tribe, the fraternity, the dojo—bonds are forged through a shared sense of mission and a dedication to it. The mission might be to practice martial arts or to confer initiatic rituals. But the very nature of the mission is that it requires not only the development of some skill but also, more especially, the development of excellence by each and every member. And excellence is closely related to presence.

The mission of a dojo might be nothing more than to teach a particular style of martial art. But it will require that its members show respect to the master, to the other students, and to anyone who might be visiting the dojo. It will require that students arrive on time. In many cases, a dojo will prohibit the use of foul language. Cleanliness of uniforms and neatness of dress might be another requirement. In other words, the dojo will have an expectation of excellence in behavior quite outside of practicing its style of martial art. And it is this practice of excellence that will cultivate presence and pride in the individual members and in the group as a whole.

Since antiquity, initiatic societies have played an essential role in the elevation of the individual to full consciousness. Somewhere around the time of puberty, the boy was put through certain ordeals or through certain rituals that transformed him into a man and into a full member of the tribe. He learned the skills he would need to survive. He learned how to endure pain or suffering. And he learned certain myths that made sense of the world. Certain crafts, too, had their own rites of initiation, and their practitioners were believed to have special powers. Blacksmiths sometimes had a semipriestly function in society, for example.

Around the twelfth century, Sufi associations in the Middle East began to be influenced by both Islamic chivalry (futuwwa) and the crafts guilds. The Sufi schools emulated the initiatic structure of the guilds, with the apprentice (*mubtadi'*), companion (*sani'*), and master craftsman (*mu'allim*). And although the stonemasons' guild of Great Britain possessed a mythology from at least circa 1400 CE and passed it down over the next few centuries with minor changes, during the early eighteenth century, it gave birth to the fraternity of Free and Accepted Masons, better known as Freemasonry (which, notably, has a similar initiatic structure of Entered Apprentice, Fellowcraft, and Master Mason).

It is true that religious and spiritual hermits have existed, but they (e.g., the Carthusians), too, have often lived in communities. There is an anecdote in the "Upaddha Sutta" of the early Buddhist Pali canon.[7] In it, the Buddha's closest disciple, Ananda, remarks to the Buddha that he believes that half of the holy life is noble friendship. This already more than suggests the essential role of a community in self-development and spiritual awakening. But upon hearing this, the Buddha responded that it is not half, but rather the whole of the holy life.

Joining is a beginning. It can take guts to walk into a martial arts school when you have no experience of fighting, just as it can to walk into a gym when you are out of shape, to join a brotherhood when you are the outsider, or to join any group when you are eager to learn but acknowledge that your level of knowledge is limited in comparison or perhaps even wrong. But that is where we all start. The point is to learn, to grow, and to share our knowledge and perspectives so that we can help the group that helped us and, we hope, help others as well.

However, it is not entirely unusual for people to seek out just enough experience to feel and to claim that they have a depth of knowledge that, in truth, they do not possess. A martial arts student might leave soon after getting his black belt. A spiritual seeker might go to a weekend workshop and shamanic initiation before heading to the office on Monday morning, believing that he has learned all there is to learn about shamanism. Or an individual might join a fraternity, take the initiation, learn the secrets, and then not return. While such people might formally possess a certain amount of skill or knowledge, they do not reflect on it or integrate it into their being. In time, their knowledge fades. In the martial arts, the body loses its muscle memory, and the kicks, blocks, and punches are forgotten. The clarity that comes with the weekend workshop out in the rain forest cannot be lived in the city. And the lessons of the initiation are forgotten.

To integrate knowledge, we must contemplate it, ask questions of those with more experience and understanding, and then contemplate it again. Moreover, we must practice the practices of the group, whether this is a martial art, a spiritual art such as meditation and prayer, or a cultural art such as painting or music. In general, we want to practice, demonstrate what we have, and get feedback on how to improve or on possibilities that might open up through our work. Perhaps a spiritual group might be able to suggest exploring certain techniques of meditation and certain authors or books or make reference to some other tradition to help the individual grow.

We might consider there to be two classifications of "individual." The mundane individual is a unit in a mass of units. He concerns himself with the things that the television and the popular culture present to him. He does not consider the big questions in life: Why am I here?

How should I live? What happens when I die? In contrast, the higher type of individual emerges only when he enters the unknown, begins to ask questions, begins to think for himself, determines to know who he is and what he should live toward, and begins to practice some kind of art—martial, spiritual, or cultural—to manifest his insights in some way or another.

It may not be impossible to do this alone, outside of any group, though it would be a very rare occurrence. Indeed, where there is real energy, there is usually a group, a partnership, or a relationship of some sort. Hence, the martial art dojo, the temple, the church, or the Sufi tariqa. And hence, Buddhists take refuge in the "three jewels" of Buddhism: the Buddha, the dharma (the teaching), and the sangha (the Buddhist community). The Bible, too, declares that "where two or three are gathered together in my name, there am I in the midst of them" (Matthew 18:20). Something happens in the group that is dedicated, with love, hope, and energy, to something higher than the individual. We might call it inspiration, but new possibilities open up for, and new qualities and strengths are often developed by, those who make up the group. Energy attracts others, and when others are actively involved, things happen.

As many "nonjoiners" realize and fear, the group submerges the identity of the individual. It gives him certain parameters, rules, restrictions that he must obey. In some cases, he must even wear certain clothes and eat only certain foods. But unlike a mass movement, such a group submerges the personality only temporarily. It is the task of the new member to learn, to remember, and to embody the rules not as restrictions but as information or as a way of being. If the group dominates his personality at first, eventually he will find his purpose and role in life through the work and dynamics of the group.

This is very much the idea of a college. One learns a skill or an art and later expands far beyond the confines of what was taught, making a new discovery in science, uncovering previously undiscovered historical evidence, or creating a new style of music or art. The purpose is not originality, per se, but rather to discover and to express one's unique being through the medium that one has come to master.

The higher type of individual chooses a group that represents a higher ideal and that will push him and guide him until he embodies that ideal. Among others, and in different ways, the guild, the initiatic society, the ancient Greek symposium, and the early Christian agape all helped the individual to transcend and to perceive the essence of reality. But groups, clubs, and societies for mutual improvement have existed throughout our history. Suggesting that its members should be "ingenious men," in 1727, along with several friends, Benjamin Franklin founded a club called the Junto or the Leather Apron Club. The twelve members, who were all artisans and thinkers devoted to learning, met on Friday evenings to discuss morals, natural philosophy, and politics. The club members were especially interested in discovering what actions and lifestyle elevated people and promoted success and, as such, should be emulated and what actions should be avoided.

The members were encouraged to discuss any knowledge they had acquired recently through reading, whether it was in relation to morality, history, engineering, poetry, or another field, or to consider anyone they knew who was either failing or succeeding in his career and life, and they would try to determine the cause of the failure or the means of success. Concerned also with society as a whole, the club members also proposed the creation of the first lending library (founded in 1731), a volunteer militia, a fire company, and a hospital.[8]

A more recent and widespread example of this type of club is the

Master Mind group inspired by the writings of Napoleon Hill. Such a group, says Mitch Horowitz in *The Power of the Master Mind*, can be composed of as few as two people and should generally not exceed seven. It exists to "support and advise" its members in the pursuit of their individual aims, though in some Master Mind groups, prayers, meditations, and visualizations play a role.[9] The format should not be complicated. At the beginning of a meeting, "a set of Master Mind principles" is read aloud. Next, each member shares some personal good news with the other members. Once everyone has shared his or her good news, each member will state what he or she is aiming to achieve over the following week. And in response, other members of the group will offer advice, suggestions, and encouragement, as well as, perhaps, applicable meditations and visualizations. Getting to the essence quickly, a Master Mind meeting should last between forty-five minutes and one hour.[10]

However, the best groups are those that are able to forge the newcomer physically and mentally so that he discovers or creates an indomitable spirit. It might be true that during this training, this initiatic period, the new member, or the "prospect," will not transcend his self, his ego, to embody a Higher Self or Spirit. Yet he has distinguished himself from his lower self, his ego, his base instincts, cravings, and fears. Through his actions, he has declared to himself that he is more— or something more essential—than all of that.

Though both the higher and lower types of individuals can submerge themselves in a group, broadly speaking, the latter does so because there is "strength in numbers," anonymity, an opportunity to feel superior because of the work of others, and approval for conforming, while the former does so, temporarily, so that his essence can be manifested and molded through his actions, like a flood of rain molding itself to a once-dried-up riverbed. Illuminating each member's strengths and weaknesses, encouraging and pushing each member to greater heights, a fellowship—if the membership is of a sufficiently high quality—is a forge for the individual who wants to become greater, to become a vehicle of the archetypal.

Yet while we are advocating the development of mind, body, and spirit, groups that are dedicated to improving all three are uncommon. There still exist martial arts schools with an unbroken lineage that draw to varying degrees on spiritual and religious practices. Besides the better known martial arts of China, Japan, and Korea, there are the Persian-, Shia-, and Sufi-influenced Zoorkhanei and the Indian, Hindu-influenced martial art of kalaripayattu. However, even in the West, some traditional Asian martial arts schools will teach meditation, healing, and some other related practices.

Some groups have emerged in recent decades that claim to teach ancient European pagan martial arts alongside some philosophy and other practices. And there are some Christian schools of martial arts. Nor should we ignore the teaching of philosophy or life lessons through the martial arts in a less formal way. Most notably, legendary boxing trainer Cus D'Amato introduced Mike Tyson to the philosophy of Friedrich Nietzsche when he was only fifteen years old.[11] And not much later, he introduced the then future world heavyweight boxing champion to Zen Buddhism and positive-thinking author Émile Coué (1857–1926).[12]

It is likely, however, that it will be necessary to cultivate different aspects of your being in different groups, combined with individual practice. You could perhaps practice a martial art in a dojo once or more a week; participate in a philosophical or spiritual discussion group once a month; and read, work out, and practice meditation alone on a daily basis. However, you should consider forming or joining a group for the purpose of self-development with those who have dedicated themselves to improving culturally, intellectually, physically, and spiritually.

Little can be achieved alone. Your group might practice physical training or martial arts and might discuss philosophy, spirituality, and culture as well, for example. Or it could simply be a discussion group composed largely of those who practice some kind of spirituality and some kind of martial art or physical training. Or in the worst case scenario, you could cultivate friendships with those who share your interest in physical, mental, and spiritual development and meet with them informally for discussions.

However, it cannot be all talk. Your group should require a certain depth of understanding and a certain level of commitment from every member and any potential member—commitment not only to the group but also to their own practice and study. It is best if the members have an understanding not only of physical training, philosophy, and spirituality, but of culture and the history of ideas as well. Yet they need not all have studied the same specific area. One might be knowledgeable about theology, another about mysticism, another about symbolism, another about art, another about literature. One might practice Brazilian jiujitsu while another might practice kung fu. This will open the minds of the participants to what is possible and will allow ideas to flow from one discipline and one practice to another.

Last, we must mention ritual. From the etiquette of the dojo to the initiation of an esoteric society and to the rites of a particular religion, ritual is a part of human expression. Although it is sometimes conflated with habit, ritual makes us more present, whereas habit is done unthinkingly, often while daydreaming about something else. Your ritual might be reading a statement of principles (such as we find in the Master Mind group) or reciting particular tenets (as in a martial arts school). It might be eating a traditional meal and giving thanks. (In regard to the latter, we have noted the ancient Greek symposium, the Christian agape, and the Table Lodge of Freemasonry, among others.) Or it might be conferring some kind of spiritual and initiatic ceremony.

Today, there are numerous tiny groups and sects that claim to be practicing ancient rituals and to possess ancient metaphysical secrets. We might wonder whether such claims are true, but ultimately, the question we should ask is not whether the rituals and secrets can be traced back to antiquity but whether the group possesses any wisdom.* Regardless of whether your group is focused on martial arts and physical health and strength, on the arts, or on philosophical discussion or is a Master Mind group, ultimately, through illuminating principles that can be found in different areas of life, it should help members come to a greater understanding, not only about the world or about themselves but also about what transcends the world and the self. As such, a group meeting should be viewed as the reembodiment of the archetypal and members should feel themselves bonded in some way—more as brothers (or brothers and sisters) than mere friends.

In the "Hávamál" (Words of the High One) of the medieval Icelandic *Poetic Edda,* we hear the advice to cultivate friendship with one we trust by speaking with him and exchanging views, through gift giving, and by visiting him often.[13] It is important to cultivate friend-

---

*Very often, such groups immerse their members in mere abstraction, conflating the symbols of one religion or mystical sect with those of another, though often distorting the meaning of one or both and without possessing any real understanding of either. Such a way of thinking becomes almost the default, as such groups rarely possess a sacred text (such as the Bible, Quran, or Bhagavad Gita) that is sufficiently complex and nuanced or that is meant to be a guide to daily life. Nevertheless, this game can appear very dazzling, since the implicit claim of the group is that it possesses the key to unlocking all of the world's secret knowledge.

ships with those whom we might think of as comrades in a struggle toward the good and toward embodying your true Self. As such, we must remove ourselves from the lives of those who drag us down, who believe that we—or even that they—cannot succeed, or who exhibit anger at the world or jealousy at others. Instead, we must make and cultivate friendships with those who are hopeful, who are full of life, who have some talent or interest that they are actively pursuing, and who genuinely want the best for us.

We have been speaking about the need to join some kind of group—a martial arts school, a group for the discussion of philosophy, and so on. Such a group is perhaps the best place to begin to make friends. But it is necessary in itself. You must have the experience of being a part of something, of struggling together with others and working toward your own betterment and the betterment of the group at the same time. And you must view your friends in the same way—not merely as people you spend time with in an act of mutual enjoyment but as people with whom you are joyfully struggling toward the good.

The struggle should be joyful because you are either succeeding in your aims or you are learning something about yourself from the struggle itself. Yet you must take time to celebrate together. Celebrate your friendship and your friend's achievements. Celebrate a cultural festival or a religious festival of importance to you. Observe the passing of time and the cycle of the years and events while recognizing that we are all mortal and are preparing our consciences as if we are about to be judged for how we have lived. Celebrate continuity and the life of the spirit that was here before you and that will live after you.

In more formal groups, such as brotherhoods or philosophical or spiritual groups or groups attached to churches or temples, the meal might—and probably should—be an established part of the culture.

The importance of the communal meal cannot be overstated. Epictetus tells us that at feasts, we entertain "two guests, body and soul."[14] For the Hindus, Father Bede Griffiths tells us that each "meal is sacred."[15] Before eating, a small amount of the food is offered to the Deity (Brahma, Krishna, Ganesha, etc.). The Divine Itself is present with those who eat together as a community.

3

THE NECESSARY WORK

FROM THE PAINTING OF ICONS by Russian Orthodox monks and nuns to the creation of mandalas with colored sand by Tibetan Buddhist monks, and from the growing of vegetables and making of wine and cheese by Benedictine and Trappist monks to the practice of the martial arts at the Shaolin temple, some kind of practical, creative work accompanies the contemplative life.

Especially in this day and age of technology and ideology, it is essential that you create something with your hands. To do so is to experience how the world works at its most fundamental level. We have to put away our theories and learn from the very things that ideologues have typically wanted to control or remake to fit their ideology: our bodies. For, contrary to the view of many intellectuals, the body is not something that can be neglected in favor of the intellect. Nor, contrary to the view of many spiritual teachers, is the body a kind of used car, meant merely to drive our soul around from point A to point B. The body matters. It is through the body that we experience the world and, therefore, come to have a sense of the miraculous or the Mystery of life and the feeling that there must be something beyond it.

It is through the body that we express our true Self. And moreover, our physical body is the alchemical laboratory in which we can test to see what kind of foods, how much physical training, how much rest, and what kind of mental attitude we need to cultivate health. For as Swami Vivekananda put it, "We want . . . muscles and nerves of steel, not namby-pamby ideas." This means that we will need humility to learn from nature—both our own nature and body and the natural world. Every ideology appears foolproof. It makes sense of everything. It explains why the world is imperfect or corrupt and how, once the principles of the ideology are applied, it will be perfected. Yet an ideology is always alien to both human nature and to nature itself. And the illusion of the perfection of the theory is shattered the moment it is applied on a large enough scale. In contrast, when we work with the hands—painting, playing a musical instrument, cooking, training our body, digging a garden, looking after a plant or an animal, and so on—we must learn from the physical.

It is common for new theories to arise that claim, for example, that we should eat certain foods that have been modified for optimal health. Generally, after some time, we discover that something was wrong with the theory, and it turns out that the whole fruit, whole egg, and so on is better for us than a food that has been modified or that had parts removed or added. Instead of theorizing, we can try to model our diet on that of our ancestors, eating natural whole foods, seeing what works for us, and cutting out what causes our body any kind of problem.

Just as food affects the way we feel physically, so, too, do ideas affect our mental stability, our emotional well-being, and our spirit or attitude. And just as we can see how we feel after eating certain food, so we can watch our thoughts to see how an idea or a belief system affects our emotions and our attitudes toward others and toward life. And we must reject those ideas and belief systems that damage us. If an idea or an ideology leads us to feel depressed, angry, or resentful; to blame others; or to feel incapable of acting on our own behalf, then we should reject it. If, however, an idea or a belief makes us feel enthusiastic, positive, loving, patient, optimistic, determined, and capable, then it is more likely to express something of our true or archetypal nature.

Practicing some kind of physical art or discipline can help us in regard to understanding our thinking, especially our preconceptions. Let's say that I want to paint a self-portrait. I do not realize it, but due to some insecurity, I have a conception of my face that is incorrect. I think I have a long nose, or big ears, small eyes, or small lips. I begin drawing my face, but then, as I look in the mirror and check the proportions, I discover that my face is not as I had thought. I have drawn my nose too long or the ears too big because of my distorted self-image. I must correct the drawing, and I must correct my own self-image.

Or I think I know how to look after a plant, but I place it where it will not get enough light. Then it withers, and I am forced to move it to where it will get sunlight. Or perhaps I think I know how to cook some particular food, but I overspice it or undercook it. Or I might believe I have mastered a martial art, but then I get punched in the face by someone with less training. In any case, I have to have the humility to think about what I did wrong and to adjust. My beliefs have to be less important than the physical nature that I am working with.

To work with the hands, to work with the body, is to engage that creative spirit—the soul, the Atman—that we identify as an aspect of the Creator of the world itself. It requires us to know how things work, to accept the quality of each thing, and to be able to work *with* all of them, rather than trying to impose our wrong ideas on reality.

Once I accept its qualities, I can focus on and develop the object of my attention, sometimes finding interesting new applications or possibilities. Hence, when people accepted that gold is too soft and too scarce to be used in the production of tools but noted that it reflected the light of the fire, it was used ritualistically and decoratively, covering the monarch's throne, for example. Noticing that the arms and other parts of the body had limitations in where and how they could move, some martial arts developed methods for subduing an opponent by manipulating his limbs in ways that were unnatural, and thus painful, or that prevented him from moving to counterattack.

The martial artist must use his own body when grappling with an opponent. When painting, using the traditional tools of ink and brush, the Chinese or Japanese artist will exhale as he makes each stroke. Polishing a mirror or cleaning and polishing a sword involved the use of the breath in the same way, and was considered a type of meditation. But we find this elsewhere. When a tailor cuts fabric, he will look in front of the shears and exhale as he slides the shears through the cloth. How the body is used is dictated by the object itself. It is the same principle.

But the body, too, must be cultivated. Plato believed physical training (gymnastic) should be taught from early childhood and that it should continue to be practiced throughout the life of the individual. However, this, he believed, had to be learned and practiced alongside music, because "exclusive devotion to gymnastic" tends to produce "a temper of hardness and ferocity," while single-minded devotion to music produces an equally undesirable "softness and effeminacy."[1]

In the West, we have come to associate the spiritual man with the figure of Jesus, at least as he has overwhelmingly been represented in Christian art: placid, passive, slender, soft, and meek. And even as Christianity has declined in many parts of the West, this image lives on in our psyches. Perhaps it seems that we are overemphasizing the physical. After all, both religion and spirituality ultimately direct our attention away from the material world and toward the Divine. But without a grounding in a physical practice, where we must face our limitations and overcome them, only to face new limitations and overcome those, it is easy to detach ourselves from reality and to fool ourselves that our quirks, fantasies, and delusions are proof of our spiritual superiority and perhaps even of psychic ability. We must wrestle with reality, as Sri Aurobindo has said, discovering infinity out of our limitations.[2]

Doubtlessly, the thin, mysterious, effeminate man in contact with spirits and immersed in dreams is one male archetype. There is something both religious and sexual—and even sexually ambiguous—about him. He is the artist, mystic, dreamer, poet, author, and sexual adventurer. He emerged in the figure of the tribal shaman who sometimes dressed in female clothes, thus presenting himself as both male and female. At once transgressing and embodying nature, it was this contradiction that gave the shaman his power to speak directly with nature and its manifestations as spirits or demons. In Norse mythology, too, we hear Odin—the god of war, magic, and poetry—being criticized for being "unmanly."[3] The basis of this accusation is Odin's practice of a feminine type of magic (*seið*), but in the modern era, we find this archetype emerging in a more British or European than American sensibility through such figures as David Bowie (especially in his Ziggy Stardust persona), the band Bauhaus, and the art of Aubrey Beardsley.

Nevertheless, this figure, like that of its opposite, the vulgar, unthinking man who trains his body but not his mind, is merely a shadowy half of what we are aspiring to be. We have not only mentioned Plato's belief that the individual should be educated and practiced in both the hard and soft arts, but we have also looked at these dual qualities in the knight, in chivalry, and in the samurai. It is this dual nature and its cultivation that provide us with a more complete and multidimensional model or archetype of the initiated or fully developed man.

"First of all our young men must be strong," said Swami Vivekananda, addressing a religious school in India in 1897. "Religion will come afterwards. . . . You will be nearer to Heaven through football than through the study of the Gita. . . . You will understand the Gita better with your biceps, your muscles, a little stronger." Why would a spiritual teacher say such a thing? Can practicing a sport or gaining physical muscle really teach us, as men, about the sacred?

A woman's body has shape, and its shape—fluid, smooth, and curvaceous—emerges through natural processes as she reaches sexual maturity. She grows into womanhood. And she grows into nature, too, her menstrual cycle timing itself to the waxing and waning of the moon and to the women around her. She does not need to work to become a woman. She is at one with nature and with the women around her. She menstruates with the other women. And when she gives birth, she is able to feed her baby with milk from her own body.

The human male is different. By itself, the young male body is often too skinny or too peachy and fleshy. The face has none of the lines that signify experience and gravitas. There is something too soft, too young, about him. The masculine body is a muscular body. And yet, a muscular body does not appear through the process of maturation alone. It can emerge only with hard, physical work—hunting with a spear, climbing, forging metal—or through physical training. But not through nature or because a boy reaches puberty.

And if the woman's cycle is aligned to that of the moon, the man is not literally aligned to its opposite, the sun. To declare himself aligned to it, he creates a world of solar symbolism: the ritual at night by the light of a flaming torch; the golden throne and crown of the king that reflect back the light of the hearth; and, later, the initiatic ritual in which the candidate enters in darkness, perhaps blindfolded, and then is exposed to light—symbolic of the "Light" of God. Yet just as he must work to become one with the sun or with the Light, so he also must sweat to achieve a man's body. In traditional cultures, this meant not only exercising but also fighting and eating and drinking with one's fellow men. In many cases, it meant some kind of relationship to animals: the horse, the dog, or perhaps on a more symbolic level, even the wolf or bear.

Take a look at the sculptures and friezes of the Acropolis: the male bodies are muscular, already hardened to life. They are machines for battle. The male makes war on horseback, the muscular body of the horse affirming the necessity of the muscular body of the warrior with whom it has become one. They are a kind of primitive, living war engine. The female sculptures are different. Their smooth, fleshy, even slightly bulbous bodies are draped in cloth that resembles water and that traces their curves. As with the female image in Indian sculpture, the breasts are emphasized; a round stomach subtly protrudes; and legs, arms, and shoulders are soft and rounded. The female bodies are sensual and relaxed.

The male is action; the female, being. In the Japanese ukiyo-e woodblock print, the samurai bursts onto the stage of life, sword in hand, grimacing, whereas the geisha sits calmly, the back of her neck suggestively exposed. Again, we see this dynamic in the giant, 160-foot-tall bronze African Renaissance monument in Senegal, a nation apparently relatively unaffected by contemporary Western intellectual trends. Inaugurated in 2010, the monument depicts a muscular African man holding an African woman, with a natural body, in one arm. In the other, he holds a young male child who is pointing at the sky and, quite possibly, to the sun.

The male must aspire. He must come to embody knowledge, skill, wisdom, and strength. But as a woman suffers in childbirth—suffers in the natural course of a woman's life—so the man must seek out a way to suffer. He must find a vocation worth suffering in and fellowship worth suffering for. He must act toward his own suffering, accepting that what emerges through discomfort is who he can be. A thinker might suffer being denounced for not surrendering to the ideological fashion of the day. The artist might suffer financial hardship or being ostracized by a community of people who disapprove of his art. A weight lifter suffers pain when he lifts weights. But the discomfort, the obstacle, the weight, that is what creates the greatness, the artistic integrity, the muscular body.

In this voluntary suffering toward an aim, the individual releases himself from the suffering forced on him in the past, especially in childhood—bullying, a lack of affection, abuse, attending a school where failure was expected and learning impossible. He accepts life as suffering but refuses the suffering inflicted on him. Refusing to be a victim, he does what he was not expected to do: he begins to forge himself anew and to forge his own destiny with it. Like the weight lifter who wakes up with his body aching from the previous day's training and is happy for it and for his vision of his life, he transforms suffering into joy.

Such an individual has begun to leave his childhood self behind and to venture into the unknown. He will have to remain calm when there is chaos, become confident, and stand upright—and stand up and be counted—when he feels that weight of uncertainty and danger pressing down on him. He cannot learn this from women. Though the infant, the baby, and even the child to some extent cleave to the mother, he must move into the realm of men. He must move into the realm of voluntary suffering for a purpose. Hence, the initiation into the male circle, embodied in its most extreme by the Spartan *agoge,* when a boy was removed from his mother at the age of seven and began a brutal regimen of training.

It is perhaps due to the double necessity of linking himself to the sun or to the Deity and making his body that of a man—a replica and an embodiment of the archetypal, primordial man—that the *männerbund* and the initiating of young men has persisted throughout the life of mankind. Thus, authentic initiation serves two functions. First, it links him to or directs him toward the solar deity or, in more monotheistic terms, to the Light, the Creator, or God. And second, psychologically and spiritually, it gives him a new body, one that is approved of and received by the initiated as being that of a fellow or brother.

There must be a uniformity of the body among the initiated. The youthful body is ceremonially, symbolically killed. Blood is spilled from it during the rite, and it is made identical, in essence, to that of the other initiates. It is a talisman that attracts the power of the sun and the blessings of the Deity, and for it to become a talisman, it must be remade to a specific, initiatic formula. Hence, in Africa, circumcision or scarification of the body form part of the initiation rite, as does tattooing among the Maori. In the former, like the newly menstruating women of the tribe, the male initiates bleed together.

Being dressed with ceremonial vestments and being secluded from the tribe (especially from the women of the tribe) usually form part of the rite. Among the Maasai, the male initiates wear black cloaks and paint their faces with white patterns. In Freemasonry, the initiate is given a white apron to wear. Traditionally, the candidate for Masonic initiation was not allowed to have any limbs missing (or to be a eunuch) since his extremities—lower legs, arms, and head—are all exposed at certain times during the initiation.*

A common sentiment among Freemasons is their sense of awe at having gone through the same initiatic experience as all of their contemporary Brothers, as well as those of the past. This is surely something that the fraternity has in common with men of other initiatic traditions. But why is this important, not only for initiates but also for a certain type of individual who cannot find meaning and satisfaction in the endless stream of entertainment, cultural fads, and political scandals that so easily preoccupy others? Why can he not—as do so many of our contemporaries—conceive of the past as a black hole with nothing of value?

"When a man has begun to be ashamed of his ancestors, the end has come," Swami Vivekananda remarked. Yet in the West, where the past is relentlessly attacked, there is hardly a people today who have not been made to feel shame at their predecessors, and few respect or revere the generations past. Yet whether we like them or not, our ancestors are in our bodies. We inherit their physical conditions, their advantages and disadvantages, their strengths, and, in some cases, their illnesses.

The contemporary Western world is in a state of rebellion against the past. "Education" criticizes the thinkers, writers, and artists of the past, who are deemed, at best, out of date. Citizens, too, criticize and even condemn the country they were born into and live in (which, for whatever reasons, they refuse to leave), and they criticize their own fam-

---

*There may be several possible interpretations of this requirement, but it is likely that it related, at one point, to the ability of the human body to form a pentagram (as Cornelius Agrippa illustrates in his *Three Books of Occult Philosophy*), which was used early on as a representation of one of the fraternity's symbols of the Deity, the Blazing Star.

ilies. No doubt we could point to another family that, if we had been born into it, would have made life easier for us. No doubt, such a family would have accepted our eccentricities, our obscure interests, and whatever else we feel is rejected by our own. But regardless, at some point we have to make peace with our family. We have to stop feeling hurt by the pain of childhood, recognizing that we have become a man or a woman and, moreover, that our family members are people like anyone else, with their own good qualities and shortcomings.

Even if we know little or nothing about our ancestors, respect for them can help us with this. We can look at things dispassionately. Perhaps we have always fought with our mother or father, but perhaps we also inherited a particular talent from or through them—a musical or artistic ability or an interest in math or language, perhaps. This talent is impersonal. It is unlikely to have begun with the parent, but it could probably be traced back generations, perhaps even hundreds or thousands of years.

Thinking about our ancestors has other benefits, too. A study published in the *European Journal of Social Psychology* showed that those who thought about their ancestors before undertaking an intellectual task both expected to do better and actually did perform better than those who thought about something else.[4] Perhaps it is unsurprising, then, that in homes of aristocrats, it was typical to find portraits not only of parents and grandparents but also of ancestors who lived further back in time. And we can see the psychological benefit, too, of tribal leaders and monarchs claiming descent from a god. Like the rest of his people, the tribal leader or monarch might have worshipped that god, but his act of worship was also an act—or a psychological trick—of remembering and revering his own ancestor and his connection to his ancestor.

Yet just as we must reconcile ourselves to our families, as far as is possible, if we choose to live there, we have to make peace with our country and its culture. This does not mean that we have to accept everything. But it means that we must find what is good in it. What is taught in schools and universities is a minuscule section of the country's culture, and whether positively or negatively, what is taught is often slanted and colored by personal prejudice or by a certain fashion in scholarship. You must see beyond the propaganda.

Just as you can acknowledge that you have inherited some talents from your mother or father, and they from theirs, and so on, so you must find what is interesting and of value to you in your culture, whether it is contemporary or from a hundred or a thousand years ago. Because there are both similarities between the cultures and influences from one to another, when you find what is of interest to you in your own, you will be able to understand other cultures better and will be able to genuinely appreciate them.

You do not have to do this for the sake of anyone else, but only for your own sake. Who is more likely to live the kind of life he wants: an individual who is full of resentment or an individual who is curious, interested, and engaged and who focuses on what brings him joy and gives him meaning? And who is more likely to be able to contribute positively to society and to the world today? Criticism infests the West. One side criticizes the past, tradition, and achievement. And the other side criticizes the critics. They have embodied, to borrow a phrase from Georg Hegel, the "negative of the negative."

They are cynics. And as philosopher Albert Camus has said, "Cynicism is homicidal."[5] Or we might say, cynicism becomes nihilism. Neither the critic nor the critic of the critic can produce anything positive, anything constructive. Sooner or later, the critic almost inevitably moves from verbal attack to literal destruction. Yet the scapegoat he beats or the government building he smashes his way into are merely symbols for him. He is estranged from the real. He acts as if in a dream. Hypnotized, he obeys the loudest and ugliest voice, which appeals to his most primitive urges. He cannot wake himself or wrestle with his conscience. Instead, he, the cynic, denounces what is good in those he imagines to be his enemies and, consequently, is forced to denounce this same good quality in himself and to retreat from the good in life, in his society, and in all societies.

Positive action requires curiosity. And when you find what is of interest in your culture and how it relates to other cultures, and when you are able to respect and appreciate your ancestors and family for passing your unique qualities to you, you erect a statue inside of your psyche to your own creative genius—to what the ancient Greeks called the *daemon*. That statue is an image, a vision, of what you are capable of or could be capable of if you dedicated yourself to a way of life that moves you.

That is the first step to becoming creative in the different areas of your life and, more importantly perhaps, to creating your own life. The mind and body shape each other. We crave a certain kind of food or are addicted to alcohol or, conversely, we want to become strong and healthy and force ourselves into the habit of physical training and eating healthy food conducive to our aim. Yet the mind shapes the body in other, subtler ways. We conceive of ourselves as strong or weak, and our body conforms to our imagination. In the short term, if we are training our body and we feel exhausted and unable to perform the exercise, visualizing ourselves doing it may push us on to complete one or two more reps. Over the long term, the way we think will shape our posture and our face.

We cannot reach our maximum potential, reason properly, or truly experience the great Mystery or wonder of life when we neglect or pollute the body. Indeed, we know that when our body is sick, we feel depressed or cannot think properly and cannot see the future clearly and with joy. When the body is weak, the individual craves safety and protection. When it is strong, the individual feels more capable of making decisions; hence, many CEOs exercise several days a week.

You must have *virtus* to have virtue. Buddhism has a notion of "nonviolence." While this means not killing animals or even insects, let's think about it only in relation to another human being. Someone tries to antagonize you into a fight, but you do not do it. Instead, you walk away. If you are weak and would have lost, you have sensibly decided not to get a beating, but there is no virtue in walking away. If you are strong, on the other hand, and could quite easily have won, you have exhibited the virtue of self-control and of not letting that person get under your skin.

For Russian philosopher and mystic P. D. Ouspensky, the average individual lacks "self-consciousness," but because he is convinced that he is self-conscious, he refuses to develop it in himself. He thinks that he acts or speaks, Ouspensky claims, but there is really only an action or speaking. Something, we might say, acts or speaks through him. What is that thing? Mostly, today it is society, or at least a large, influential section of society. Hence, he changes his opinion as the rest of society changes its opinion. A long-held opinion gives way overnight, not only in the ordinary man but also among politicians. Sensing that opinion has changed on an emotive issue, even the president of a country will sometimes change his mind and go with the flow. (Few know themselves well enough or hold any values or beliefs strongly enough to be able to resist.)

The individual conforms to the mass, and the mass conforms to itself, adjusting as quickly as possible to the most powerful (i.e., those capable of influencing others to expel an individual from a particular group—friends or a place of employment—or from the mass as a whole). As we noted earlier on, to be exiled in tribal society was a punishment only slightly less severe than execution. And the fear of being exiled remains with us. The average individual either does not question or questions only so that he can find the reason that the mass or the mob is right and why he should conform.

Yet there is another type of individual: one in which the archetypal speaks through him; not every archetype equally, but one that gives his life structure and symbolic value that outweigh the awesome symbolic power—the display of brute force—of the mob. At one with the gods or heroes, he is not alone in facing the mob. Nor is he submerged and lost in the archetypes. Rather, he is at one with them. He draws on their myths and he draws on the biographies of the great historical figures to give him the strength to become conscious of who he is and to live as he believes he should.

Often, the individual experiences self-realization when he does what he believes is least important about himself: cooking, gardening, fixing an engine, painting a picture, going for a walk in nature, or practicing some hobby. He considers it the least important thing about himself because it is to the side of his connection to society; it is not part of his job or marriage, nor does it express his political or religious affiliation. It is a "break" or a way of "turning off" for a short while. Yet it is precisely its detachment from social pressure that makes it of value. No less important, he loves doing this activity. It is who he truly is, as far as he has developed himself.

Recognizing the potential of such ordinary activities and ordinary moments, Zen Buddhism in Japan elevated the arts along with the simplest of tasks to that of the Way—an expression of the Tao. Probably the most well-known and admired martial artist of the last hundred years, Bruce Lee studied *wing chun* and other Chinese martial arts, as well as Western boxing and fencing. But early on, he also took up cha-cha dancing, becoming the Hong Kong cha-cha champion in 1958. And of course, while we often see them as opposites, dance and martial arts are related in many cultures, from the *umzansi* (war dance) of the Zulus to capoeira, the Brazilian martial and acrobatic art that is performed to the music of the *berimbau* (bow), *atabaque* (drum), and other instruments.

For Ayn Rand, man, who is unable to rely on instinct as other animals are able, survives because he is rational—and the rational man finds his purpose in "productive work."[6] Her message is the Protestant work ethic minus the Christian sense of something beyond this world. And despite her being fervently anti-Communist, it shares something of Communism's emphasis on "production" and on the notion of each working according to his ability and needs, though the Randian gets to keep the fruits of his labor while the Communist rarely has. In Zen Buddhism and in other traditions and cultures less consciously, perhaps, the arts and daily tasks offer the possibility of self-transcendence. The individual does not find meaning in the work, per se, but turns it into a meditation. Polishing a mirror or sweeping leaves, the Zen Buddhist focuses on the breath, quiets the normally chattering mind, and experiences a certain stillness of being.

Another problem of Rand's philosophy is its broad rejection of instinct and the nonrational. Historically, man used his instinct. (He still does.) Instinct was essential to the hunting party and war band. It has remained essential for the artist, martial artist, entrepreneur, and even, on occasion, the scientist. The ability to think nonrationally is, as unconventional marketing guru and author Rory Sutherland has observed, essential to invention, marketing, and even the military. If, after all, a military commander always does the rational thing, he will be predictable, and being predictable, he will be easy to defeat. Hence, the military leader, like the artist, must be able to think nonrationally.

We must be able to think rationally, too, of course. And rational thinking requires us to be honest and to resist twisting the facts to suit our ideology or hurt feelings, which modern man seems increasingly incapable of. But we do not want the rational to become our entire world. And although we want to be productive, our entire lives cannot be a matter of "productivity." Ultimately, we are suprarational, and we find meaning in the body; in the landscape; in sex, love, spirituality, ritual, family, brotherhood, friendship, and so on. And we are nourished by beauty and by what transcends the productive. We are awakened by the sight of a beautiful woman or a beautiful landscape or when visiting a museum and seeing paintings or sculptures that embody the beauty, glory, wonder, and struggle of life.

The suprarational man finds his Self emerging from the archetypal, through mind, body, and spirit and through the emergence of the transcendent: beauty, strength, and wisdom. Hence, the European gentleman learned the seven liberal arts as well as the art of the sword for self-defense; the samurai studied the art of war but also, perhaps, calligraphy, poetry, and painting; and the Confucian studied philosophy, ritual, archery, and so on.* They studied the arts of war and peace. They studied what expanded their consciousness far outside that of the ordinary man, whether productive or unproductive, rational or superstitious.

---

*In more recent times, world heavyweight boxing champion Lennox Lewis was also a dedicated chess player.

We have already come across the classical Chinese and Japanese idea of a Way—the practice of an art (from painting to martial arts) through which an individual can reach a new level of spiritual understanding. While in the West, the arts are not typically thought of as connected to the spiritual, if someone is artistically inclined but does not pursue it, very often he will come to express great frustration and anger in later life. And if such a person takes up politics, he often becomes idealistic, dogmatic, uncompromising, technical, cold, and inhuman. In contrast, when the thinker or the spiritual man adopts an art and pursues it, he not only sees his skill improve but also finds that his sensitivity to the world develops—and it develops because he is involved in the act of creating. Nicholas Roerich and Frithjof Schuon were both spiritual teachers who developed a high degree of technical proficiency in painting as well as a large body of work. And the art styles of Piet Mondrian, Wassily Kandinsky, and Jackson Pollock were all shaped, to a degree, by the once-influential but now little-known spiritual school of Theosophy.

Nevertheless, over the last century, entrepreneurship has not infrequently been infused with the ideas of the positive thinking movement, or New Thought, which emphasizes the power of imagination, integrity, self-improvement, knowing oneself, and doing what is in line with one's true nature or interests. Moreover, the positive thinking movement is fundamentally metaphysical and believes that we can align ourselves with the Divine and gain the help of the Divine by constantly imagining and projecting ourselves, mentally, into our ideal future. However, this should be practiced in tandem with actually working toward one's aims and working to address issues in one's own psyche, habits, and so on.

Most of us need to work. Yet it is important to attempt to find work that enables us to express our talents or inclinations and that is both challenging and rewarding. However, whether this is or is not possible, take up a practice, or practices, that you can develop over time—painting, writing, playing an instrument, public speaking, woodwork, or some other art or skill. Find something that you can become skilled in and that can help you to understand the inherent creativity of the world. Cultivate discipline. Create a routine. Simplify your life by focusing on what matters to you. But understand that discipline, routine, and simplicity are not punishments but what help us to know ourselves, to develop ourselves, and to create what is of value to us and what might be of value to others living in our own time and facing similar challenges to us.

Moreover, cultivate the seemingly opposing aspects of your being. Practice poetry and physical strength, art, and martial arts; study classical philosophy and popular culture; study within a tradition but invent and create. The point of a tradition is that the practitioner can draw on the work and insights of masters from centuries past. These masters have thought through the tradition and its limitations, advancing its technique and understanding. The modern practitioner, then, has a body of work and advanced ideas to work through. With a tradition, he does not need to begin at the beginning.

Yet as it is foolish to throw away a tradition in the arts, in philosophy, in theology, in spirituality, or in ritual—casting oneself into the nihilism of the moment—so you must not mistake the substance for the essence. What matters is the energy—the living, creative spirit—of the tradition. Whatever was created should serve as a source of inspiration and not as an object of worship. Tradition and innovation must be balanced. And they must be continually rebalanced in a society that swings from one extreme to the other. Thus, when tradition is attacked, that is what must be defended, and when innovation and creativity are attacked, they must be defended.

There is, however, a vital aspect of tradition that is rarely mentioned. Tradition not only provides a foundation, it provides, also, a target. A philosopher or artist, for example, adopts aspects of his predecessors' work but rejects and opposes other elements of it. Doubtlessly, just as there can be dull obedience to tradition, so also can extreme and unthinking opposition produce work that is no less dull and lifeless, even if it is wrapped in the veneer of rebellion and radical thought. Opposition within a tradition has to emerge out of deep and lengthy contemplation.

As we have already advocated, it is better to develop both the body and the intellect, for if one is neglected, your being will be out of balance. Yet it is not necessarily the case that the neglected aspect will fade from view. It might, in fact, take over. It might be different for each person, but often, those who do not train the body find their aggression manifesting through their intellect. Those who neglect the gut, refusing to take risks, are hypersensitive to every little trial or tribulation and believe that they are in a constant battle. Those who do not cultivate the heart fall in love with themselves.

4

FROM OBSTACLE TO ACCOMPLISHMENT

EVERY FIELD HAS ITS EXPERTS. But expertise is not mastery. And technical knowledge is not wisdom. Counterintuitively, perhaps, mastery of an art first requires one to be totally mastered by it. To become a master musician, one must first adapt to the instrument. If one wishes to be a master of a martial art, one must adapt to both the techniques and the physical demands, enduring pain, bruises, and perhaps other injuries and watching as the body changes and develops over time. The same occurs with the mind. The student must become conscious of his weaknesses and strengths, not only in regard to technique but also in regard to himself as a person and in regard to his mind, body, and spirit. Unnecessary for expertise, humility is a condition of mastery.

Innovation is not an entirely conscious process, however. It is more like a dream that we dream, unaware that it is occurring within us. Distinct and different things merge together unconsciously during a period of incubation; then the idea appears like a revelation or a flash of inspiration. This is something quite beyond technical production and beyond cleverness. Most authors and artists understand the necessity of leaving a project aside for a time to allow it to incubate. The work has to be forgotten about and then returned to. Sometimes a flash of inspiration—the answer to the puzzle—comes when the individual has forgotten about it. At other times, looking at it afresh will reveal strengths and weaknesses. If an individual takes an interest in an array of different fields, his consciousness will evolve, at times seeming to take leaps of imagination or thinking to come up with novel ideas.

In ancient tribal societies, certain individuals were initiated into the Mysteries either in their dreams or through a life-altering sickness. Dreaming, such an individual peered into the spirit world that lay outside of ordinary vision but that nonetheless permeated reality and that was, in some sense, the essence of reality, expressing those laws that had to be obeyed or worked with to ensure the tribe survived and flourished. Upon becoming a shaman, he could communicate with these spirits or with the tribal gods and goddesses, appealing to them for help—to heal the sick, to bring rain, or to give the tribe a good harvest. Sickness or temporary madness, too, could produce visions. And both dreaming and sickness set these individuals apart from the rest of the community, yet, crucially, the community—the tribe—had a role for them. These were the visionaries who communed with gods and spirits or were healers.

As we have said, ancient tribal initiations were often brutal. Male Maasai youths were circumcised without any form of anesthetic. And to scream or cry out in pain brought shame to the individual, who would be marked out as a coward. Among the Spartans, boys had to live as if feral, away from the rest of the population, fending for themselves for survival, having to kill animals and steal food to survive; in the latter case, they risked being whipped by Spartan warriors who stood guard.

Even in later initiations, such as that of Freemasonry, we find such symbols as the skull and crossbones, sword, and dagger.

This might strike you as barbaric and unnecessary. But despite the presence of initiating elders, the initiate is self-made. He encounters adversity, whether physical or psychological, and overcomes it. Yet despite our society's growing desire for more and more safety, a kind of spontaneous shamanic initiation can still occur, setting in motion a transformation of the individual's psyche or aims in life. Hence, even in our secular age, the metaphysical permeates much of our culture: consider Jungian psychology, movies that retell ancient myths or that create new ones, and the adoption of occult symbols and motifs in popular music and fashion.

You, too, may have felt somehow different from those around you, either because you have dreamed bigger or dreamed differently or because of some inherent difference in your sense of reality or even your physical nature. Such a feeling can be overwhelming and can make you feel very negatively about yourself and about the world. In childhood, because of your difference, you may have found yourself ostracized, bullied, demeaned by parents or teachers, or dismissed as a fool, a failure, or a freak. Or perhaps even more dangerous, you might have been lavished with sympathy because of your apparent weakness, and, in turn, you might have begun to crave that sympathy, to crave the attention of the sick child.

This is one of the most enticing dangers of the contemporary era: to see oneself as a victim of circumstance, incapable of mustering the will to change one's own life and simultaneously being at the mercy of and in need of the help of others—parents, activists, governments, NGOs—mythologizing our suffering through politics. Regardless of the faith, religious people have been more immune to such thoughts because they generally believe that periods of suffering are punishment for some misdeed (which can be atoned for), God testing the individual and preparing him for greatness, or karma.

Regardless of how you may have been treated in the past, you must recognize in your difference a source of strength and creativity rather than weakness and limitation. This does not mean using your "weakness" to get special treatment. It means being able to look at and to ponder the life-puzzle that your early struggles have given you. Individuals looking to find a career path are often advised to consider the things they were good at and enjoyed as a child. But you should also consider the things you struggled with and that might even have made you feel embarrassed. Try to recall your challenges. Do not look back with any sense of self-pity, but do so to discover your resilience and to remind yourself of those things you felt important enough to struggle with. There you will find clues to who you are or who you can become. As you will see, many—perhaps most—of the innovators in society have come from difficult backgrounds, suffered sicknesses or serious accidents, or had learning difficulties. It did not stop them. In many cases, a line can be drawn directly from the early struggle to the greatness of the individual.

The innovator, the artist, raises his work from technical proficiency to mastery by imbuing it with that indefinable quality sometimes referred to as "heart" or "soul." Nevertheless, things take time to mature, and understanding and wisdom lag considerably behind experience. The early work of creators is usually little more than a copy of those who have gone before them. Then something happens. They go beyond the technique, innovate, and create something relevant to their own time. "As iron sharpens iron, so one man sharpens another," says Proverbs,[1] so the art and the disciple of the art sharpen each other. First, the art sharpens the disciple. Then, having achieved mastery, he sharpens the art. First, it gives him new expression, then he gives it new expression. But this is not a mere reversal. The master brings his experience—his life experience, his gravitas—to the art, including insights that he has drawn from other areas of his life.

In our own time, however, human potential is being reevaluated. Success and failure are increasingly seen as having less to do with individual choices and actions than with the society the individual was born into. Our choices ultimately don't matter much or are predetermined by social conditions, it is suggested. The debate as to whether we have free will or our lives are predetermined is an ancient one. In religion, the belief that God has determined everything that has happened, is happening, or will happen is called predestination. Likewise, astrology views our lives as predetermined—at least to a considerable degree—by the movements of the planets. Today, though, if a person is successful, it is not because of God or because of an individual's rising sign but, it is increasingly believed, because "the system" has worked for him. And if someone is unsuccessful, it is because "the system" has worked against him. That is where it ends. You, me, and everyone else are conceived of as both products manufactured by the machinery of society, which is believed to be in need of rewiring if we are all to be more alike and more equal, and as cogs in that same machine.

Perhaps the most eloquent and sophisticated version of the claim comes from *New York Times* best-selling author Malcolm Gladwell. He claims that, as a society, we regard success as being "exclusively" the result of "individual merit." However, Gladwell argues, when and where we are born and grow up largely determines who we will become and what we will achieve. He points out, for example, that like most early computer pioneers, Bill Gates and Steve Jobs were both born in

1955. And adding to the luck of being born in the optimal year, Jobs lived close to Silicon Valley and was exposed to its engineers from an early age. As a schoolchild, Jobs even managed to get Bill Hewlett of Hewlett-Packard to give him some spare computer parts to tinker with, along with a summer job on the company's assembly line.[2]

But it's not just the year that matters. In some cases, it's also the month. Illustrative of this, the majority of major league baseball players were born in August, Gladwell notes.[3] But why should that matter? It's simple. The cutoff date for selection is July 31. So a child born in August will have to wait to the following year's tryouts to see if he can make the team selection. But this means he will be more experienced and more mature at the time of the tryouts, giving him a small but significant advantage over other hopefuls born later in the year. Nevertheless, there are plenty of professional baseball players who were born in July and throughout the rest of the year. And while Jobs became perhaps the most admired, emulated, and referenced entrepreneur of the modern age, particularly for his work with Apple, we do not hear anything about others born in or near Silicon Valley in 1955. Why not? Shouldn't we be able to reverse-engineer the theory and, with little more than a birth date and location (and perhaps with class and gender as well), be able to pick out the winners and losers of history? Clearly, that doesn't work. And Gladwell acknowledges that the background of an individual is not the sole factor. Rather, it provides the foundation for success or lack of success. If someone is born at the right time and at the right place and if he is willing to "work really hard,"[4] this combination will—or will likely—propel him to success.

This seems to make a lot of sense. After all, if Jobs had been born a few decades later, personal computing would already have become popular and someone else might have launched a brand like Apple. Or if he had been born a few decades earlier, computers would have been rare and extremely expensive, and Jobs would almost certainly not have had the opportunity to experiment with such technology as a child or to meet and listen to computer engineers. Or what if Jobs had grown up in an impoverished neighborhood? Or in a third world country? Probably, we would never have heard of him.

But still, why Jobs? He was adopted. He struggled at school. And he dropped out of college. This doesn't spell success. Jobs was also interested in Buddhism and went on the hippie trail. Then, after officially dropping out of Reed College, he took lessons under a Trappist monk named Robert Palladino in perhaps the world's most outdated and outmoded art: calligraphy.[5] This is the sketch of a man who is a dreamer, a dabbler in an arcane art, and destined for failure, not success.

Being born in the right place and time plus the ability and willingness to "work really hard" will almost certainly enable the individual to enjoy a certain amount of success in a particular career. And if he is born into a family with money and connections as well, he will likely amass an amount of wealth far beyond the expectations of the average person. But unless the Fates force him to confront serious adversity (and, consequently, to confront himself), he will never be a Steve Jobs, nor an Elon Musk, nor a Vincent van Gogh, a Jean-Michel Basquiat, a Frida Kahlo, a David Bowie, or a Steven Spielberg. (He will never, in fact, become himself.) And if it isn't already clear, this book is not concerned with the insider. It is concerned with the outsider. It is concerned with the rebel, the misfit, the innovator, the disruptor, the visionary, with the revolutionary who does not spit on culture and tear society down but brings something of quality to it—leadership, inspiration, vision, an art, an aesthetic, a quality, a way of seeing things, integrity, strength of character—and reminds us of some integral part of our nature. And of course, this book is concerned with your potential for inner revolution: to become who you truly are deep down and should be.

It is the ability to triumph over disadvantages or to turn them into advantages that largely determines whether an individual becomes a leader, a trailblazer, and a revolutionary in a field, or perhaps invents a whole new field. An easy life rarely produces such notables. Jobs's study of calligraphy must have seemed like a joke. But it was those studies that gave him the idea to put different fonts into Apple computers. Yes, in hindsight, the decision seems obvious to us, because we are used to different fonts in technology, but at the time it was revolutionary and it was a stroke of genius. Before Apple, all computers had used a calculator-type font, often in green on a black screen. And since calculators (like typewriters) had never changed their font, there was no reason to think computers would, or should, either.

For argument's sake, let's just accept that being born in 1955 and living around Silicon Valley engineers, at the very least, Jobs was likely to become professionally involved in computing. But was he likely to take a class in calligraphy? No. Going by the date and place of his birth, it is extremely unlikely that Jobs would have learned the arcane and long-outmoded art. And was he likely to revolutionize computing by introducing the medieval art to modern technology or to remake the image of computing by introducing a definitely minimalist, Zen Buddhist aesthetic to it? Probably not. In fact, what made Jobs unique was not his advantages but his disadvantages. Or to put it another way, it was not being an insider but being an outsider that enabled him to think creatively, take risks, and become the world leader in modern technology.

Here we have to ask: If we can predict success on the basis of an individual's birth date and where he or she grew up, then why did many of the most influential figures of our society grow up in difficult circumstances or have some serious illness or learning disability? Singer, songwriter, and musician Johnny Cash and rapper and entrepreneur 50 Cent were both born into poverty, as were many celebrities. These were people born in the wrong place at the wrong time, surely. But the list goes on. Axl Rose, the singer of Guns N' Roses, was subjected as a child to frequent beatings by his stepfather.[6] Actor Charlize Theron's father was an alcoholic who made life unpredictable and dangerous. (Things got so bad that when Theron was fifteen years old, her father attacked her mother, who shot and killed him in self-defense.)[7] Similarly, Gordon Ramsay's father was a severe alcoholic who took his frustration out on Gordon's mother.[8] The family was also always on the move, and Gordon attended seventeen different schools by the age of sixteen.[9] At fifteen, Ramsay began pursuing a career as a soccer player and trained with the Rangers soccer team in Scotland for a few months, but he suffered leg injuries that put him out of the game.[10] Yet, despite these and other very considerable challenges, Ramsay pushed himself relentlessly, becoming probably the world's best-known chef.

Again, Virginia Woolf and F. Scott Fitzgerald were two of many authors to have battled depression. George Orwell suffered a childhood bacterial infection that left him with damaged bronchial tubes (and not unrelated to that, he was dying of tuberculosis when he was writing his masterpiece, *1984*).[11] Fyodor Dostoevsky had epilepsy. Michael Phelps, Michael Jordan, and many other star athletes have ADHD.[12]

As a child, John F. Kennedy was bedridden with scarlet fever; suffered a range of ailments from digestive problems to infections, measles, mumps, whooping cough, and bronchitis; and was hospitalized for what doctors feared might be leukemia.[13] Theodore Roosevelt was severely afflicted with asthma, with attacks often lasting days on end.[14]

Baldwin IV, king of Jerusalem, contracted leprosy as a child. Though it is usually a fatal disease, Baldwin managed to live on and, as king, led his Crusader army from victory to victory, despite only being able to hold a sword in his left hand, since his right was numb from the disease.[15]

These are just a few examples of many. But looking at them, we have to ask, Why does there often appear to be a link between the childhood affliction—or, at the very best, youthful struggles and rejection—and the later success? Kennedy's mother, Rose, thought that her son's childhood sicknesses might have given "him another kind of strength that helped him to be the great man he became."[16] Certainly, Roosevelt fought back against his sickness, taking up weight training to strengthen his body and, of course, forging his character at the same time.

But did these men and women really become celebrities, writers, innovators, presidents, and leaders partly because of their disadvantages and afflictions? Or despite them? Suffering with extreme anxiety throughout his life, Norwegian artist Edvard Munch was in no doubt. "Without this illness and anxiety," he said, "I would have been like a ship without a rudder."[17] The illness and the miseries he had experienced became his guides. And without any doubt, Munch had experienced many miseries, suffering not only poverty as a child but also enduring the death of his mother and older sister, Sophie. Yet as an artist, he was able to pour his suffering into his dark, intensely colored, gloomy but powerful paintings, including, of course, his best-known work, *Der Schrei der Natur,* or *The Scream.*

If Munch found direction and purpose through his suffering, the German philosopher Friedrich Nietzsche found strength. He proclaimed, "What does not kill me makes me stronger."[18] And with good reason. This has to be the attitude of anyone who is struggling to succeed in a world where he is an outsider and in a world that he will shock and shake up if he is successful. Ernest Hemingway said, "The world breaks everyone and afterward many are strong at the broken places."[19] Some, not all.

Why didn't all the people we've mentioned so far, and those we'll soon look at, just give up, drown themselves in drugs or drink, or turn into resentful, vengeful people intent on hurting others or hurting themselves? First, they each found a creative outlet, expressing or transcending their inner torment and conflict through writing, acting, painting, or music. Recognizing that the mind was the ultimate tool, they worked on themselves—on their thinking—as they worked on their skills. Second, their desire to do good ultimately trumped any sense of self-pity or desire for revenge that they might have felt. They wanted to transform their own lives, to develop the Will—or willpower—to keep going through difficult times and to get away from the source of their suffering, but they also wanted to improve the lives of others or to inspire others in some way.

Having confronted the struggles of your past, do not become attached to them; do not make it all about you. See things from the outside. If a parent or childhood friend hurt you, it is not because he or she was uniquely evil and powerful but because that person had his or her own unresolved emotional issues, or perhaps even psychological issues, which probably began during childhood. Understand that this person did not act out of strength, but out of weakness. Such people are not powerful; they are weak. Do not be like them. Instead, act, work, or create with the intention of empowering others, enabling them to see how it is possible for them to overcome their own internal struggles and self-limiting beliefs. Perhaps this will mean creating some kind of art or product or service, or perhaps it will mean mentoring on a one-to-one basis or improving the culture of your company. Most likely, being an integral part of who you are, it will take different forms and will change over time as you yourself grow and your skills develop.

Perhaps you have felt resentful or jealous of others' success in the past, or perhaps you still do. You must also work to change this. There are really three emotional responses to seeing someone who embodies qualities that you would like to have: jealousy, admiration, and inspiration. With the first two responses, there is no attempt to work toward bettering oneself, though the jealous person feels bad about it and the admiring individual feels pleasure. Only those who are inspired set to work to change themselves. And this can be an ongoing, lifelong task.

Jealousy is a reflection of fear and self-doubt. There is a strength in feeling genuinely happy for the success and self-development of others. When you are genuinely happy for another's good fortune, you affirm to yourself—perhaps subconsciously—that you, too, have what it takes and that you, too, are taking positive action and working toward your own goals. Turn jealousy into admiration and admiration into inspiration. Take positive action. Consider this: You and the other person are both moving up, though, of course, good news will not arrive for you both at the exact same time. But it is happening for both of you because you are both working toward a better life. Work, determination, adaptability, and learning have to be married to persistence or "grit."

If you haven't started, think about the areas in your life that need improving. Beginning is generally the most difficult stage. Start small but create a routine, work on it every day, and dedicate more time to it as you progress. Whether it's gaining muscle or losing weight, developing a new skill, practicing an art, working on relationships, or developing your career, be conscious of and appreciate even small signs of success. These will help you to continue. To expand on Nietzsche's now famous comment, what does not kill us makes us not only stronger but also driven, more adaptable, inquisitive, willing to try different things, less afraid of looking foolish, and more confident that we can—if we try—affect real change in our lives. You are no longer the wounded child but the man who is capable of striking out on his own.

People who cannot or will not take manageable risks—risks that they can, in fact, afford to take—remain stunted by past experiences. They are broken or fragile. But having faced the puzzle and the pain within you, you can find a source of inner strength. Philosopher and author Nassim Nicholas Taleb has given a name to the phenomenon. The opposite of fragile, he calls it "antifragile." While the fragile people break and the robust endure and remain the same, antifragile people "benefit from shock."[20] Stressors, disorder, randomness, and volatility all help the antifragile to grow. Take weight training. Lifting heavy weights stresses the muscles, causing small tears in the tissue. Or to put it a little more dramatically, it damages the tissue. When you rest and recuperate, the body works to repair the tears and strengthens them, causing an increase in muscle density. A hurricane may damage many trees, but because nature is antifragile, plant life benefits from the hurricane, which can scatter seeds of new plant life across an area of thousands of miles.

A culture that is antifragile will benefit from new ideas or techniques, being affected by them, and reshaping and injecting new life into aspects of the culture—hence, for example, the influence of Japanese woodblock print on French Impressionism. In fact, new and powerful subcultures are often born out of dire circumstances: in music, blues, punk, and hip-hop were all born in a background of poverty and social strife. Punks usually purchased cheap, used clothes and cut them up, painted on them, or put safety pins through them. Punk bands often only knew a few basic chords on the guitar, but the rudimentary sound they created was new and, in contrast to the highly polished sounds of disco, spoke to a disenfranchised generation. Early hip-hop often relied on "spinning" existing records together to make new music. Graffiti artists sprayed subway trains in New York City instead of showing their work in prestigious galleries. And break dancers laid broken-down cardboard boxes on the street for their dance floor. They did not need expensive equipment to create something new.

We have mentioned several remarkable individuals who shaped our culture after wrestling with serious illnesses, poverty, or instability in their childhood or youth. But let's consider dyslexia. Five to 15 percent of Americans suffer from the learning disability.[21] Surely, we would expect the number to be lower among high achievers in the world of business. Yet it is far higher. In fact, a staggering 35 percent of entrepreneurs in the United States[22] are dyslexic—Charles Schwab and Kevin O'Leary among them.[23] Dyslexia is an especially interesting disadvantage for entrepreneurs because self-made, wealthier individuals tend to see reading as essential to a lifelong process of self-education and, consequently, read more books than less wealthy individuals.[24] To put it more succinctly, an entrepreneur is more likely to have a "reading disability" and more likely to read more books than the average individual. Logically, this should not be the case.

Is a disadvantage really an advantage from a different perspective? Charles Schwab has said that having dyslexia meant he was able to look at things differently, come up with novel ideas, and "conceive of things more quickly than other people could."[25] Disadvantage necessitates inventiveness. It requires going off the beaten track. And perhaps as a survival mechanism for the ego, it stimulates daydreaming, causing the individual to immerse himself in the imaginal world. There could be other advantages, too. While dyslexics can struggle with small—if often important—details, dyslexic entrepreneurs, at least, are able to see the big picture when others are not. And while dyslexics struggle with written language, they are often superior verbal communicators who are able to articulate their vision to those they are with.[26] And superior verbal communication requires an understanding of the emotional power of words; how sentences should be structured for maximum impact; and how to read, connect with, and inspire an audience.

But if dyslexia is overrepresented among entrepreneurs, autism is overrepresented in the tech industry. And this seems to have been the case even early on. In 1984 psychologist Jean Hollands wrote a self-help book for women who were in a relationship with or married to men who were suffering from what she called "silicon syndrome" (after Silicon Valley), a condition that Steve Silberman points out has all the characteristics of Asperger's syndrome, which is now generally regarded as a subtype of autism.[27] Having difficulty perceiving social cues, struggling with social interactions, focusing intensely on a subject of interest, being detail oriented, and having a determination to take a purely rational approach to every aspect of life are some of the qualities of autism. And in some situations and professions, of course, logic and an intense focus on details can be extremely valuable.[28]

It isn't difficult to find media speculation that prominent leaders in the tech industry (as well as in other industries) have been on the autism spectrum, and a few celebrities have been diagnosed with high-functioning autism. Singer and musician Courtney Love was diagnosed as "mildly autistic" as a child.[29] And Gary Numan, one of the pioneers of electronic music in Great Britain, was diagnosed with Asperger's syndrome as a youth. He believes it was an "advantage," giving him the "concentration and obsession" necessary to succeed, even if it made social interactions more awkward.[30] Indeed, far from allowing the condition to hold him back, Numan greatly enlarged on the Asperger's type personality for his stage persona, intentionally appearing cold and aloof, never smiling or making eye contact, and singing about cars, technology, and electricity and not so much about romance.

Illnesses and learning disorders are disadvantages that some exceptional individuals manage to turn to their advantage. Others have had to wrestle with serious accidents or injury during childhood or to confront death. The renowned Mexican artist Frida Kahlo (1907–1954) made her first painting as she lay in bed recovering from a bizarre and life-threatening accident. Before then, she had planned to become a doctor. The accident occurred on September 17, 1925. Kahlo and her boyfriend, Alejandro Gómez Arias, were taking a bus home from school when it collided with a tram. The force of the impact split the tram in half. Kahlo was impaled on a metal handrail (which broke her spine and pelvis and exited through her vagina) and thrown from the bus. The force of the collision also stripped Kahlo of her clothes, and when Gómez Arias found her, she was lying naked, though covered in blood as well as gold glitter, which another passenger on the bus had been carrying.[31]

Several people were killed, and it was uncertain whether Kahlo would survive. She spent a month in the hospital, unable to do anything except lie in bed, and a further two months confined to bed at home. After this, Kahlo was forced to wear a series of different plaster cast corsets that restricted her movements and would not allow her to sit up, and with this and suffering from permanent exhaustion, Kahlo still spent much of the time in bed. A year after the accident, she was readmitted to the hospital. Despite the horrific nature of her injury, the doctors had not x-rayed her spine. Now it was discovered that several of her vertebrae had been displaced.[32]

Yet it was during this time of physical pain, exhaustion, and severe physical restriction that Kahlo left behind her ambition of becoming a doctor and initiated her life as an artist. Using a specially constructed easel made for her by a local carpenter at her mother's request, Kahlo painted as she lay in bed. Her first work was a portrait of a friend. A canopy, with a mirror fixed to its underside, was added to the bed so that Kahlo could see her reflection and could use herself as her own model. And it is for her self-portraits that Kahlo would become famous and is still known today.

We mentioned David Bowie earlier. Like Kahlo, Bowie suffered an injury as a youth, and it was one that would affect his self-image and, ultimately, who he would become and how the adult star would be seen by the world. As teenagers, Bowie and his friend George Underwood (who would become Bowie's lifelong artistic collaborator) were both attracted to the same girl, and Bowie began boasting about his sex appeal. Angered, Underwood punched Bowie in the left eye. He hadn't hit the future singer and performer hard, but his nail scraped Bowie's eyeball, paralyzing the muscle responsible for opening and closing the iris. Bowie's left iris stayed permanently wide open, giving the impression that he had two different colored eyes.[33]

Bowie (then David Robert Jones) could have been forgiven for thinking that his strange appearance would make a career as a performer impossible. But instead, the strange, enigmatic, and otherworldly look became integral to Bowie the performer, who, early in his career, presented himself through a number of characters, the most notable of which was Ziggy Stardust (1972–1974). Thin and pale, as Stardust Bowie added to the strangeness of his appearance by dying his hair red and painting a red and blue lightning flash around his right eye. The theme of his music was also alien: the songs "Starman" and

"Life On Mars," and the album *The Rise and Fall of Ziggy Stardust and the Spiders from Mars*. Only a few years later, in 1976, Bowie starred in the science fiction film *The Man Who Fell to Earth*, playing the role of an alien who crash-lands his spaceship on Earth with the hope of transporting a vast amount of water back to his planet, which is suffering from severe drought.

There are few explicit references to mysticism or the occult in Bowie's lyrics. In his song "Quicksand," recorded in 1971, he refers to the British, Victorian-era occult society called the Hermetic Order of the Golden Dawn and to Britain's most notorious, colorful, and publicity-seeking occultist Aleister Crowley. But such references are less interesting than Bowie's stage personas and his attempt to portray himself as a kind of shamanic priest for the space age. And they are less interesting because they are more obvious, more literal. Although less flamboyant, Bowie's alienness is still evident in his later work, especially, perhaps, in *Heathen* (released in 2002) and his final album, *Blackstar* (released in 2016).

We have already looked at serious illnesses and accidents among those who would go on to become innovators and, in some cases, celebrities. However, some came face-to-face with their mortality as a child or youth or, at least, before their careers had bloomed. This is perhaps especially significant, as the theme of mortality is prominent in shamanic and other initiations, including initiation into the Freemasonic fraternity today. In the latter case, the candidate for membership is sometimes left in a dark room called the Chamber of Reflection. In it is placed a skull and crossbones, and on the walls are written various statements. Sometimes this includes the following: "If you want to live well, think of death."[34] But why? A close encounter with death, whether real or enacted, makes the individual think about what is important in his or her life. How much sex you've had or how much money you've amassed won't be what's on your mind as death approaches. Instead, you will think of the people you love and what you achieved in your life—what legacy you leave behind. Or maybe you will think about what's beyond this world.

Let's briefly consider the Serbian-born scientist and inventor Nikola Tesla (1856–1943). Although somewhat sidelined in the history of science, Tesla inspired many in the scientific community during his own time, and, on his seventy-fifth birthday, was congratulated by many scientists, including Albert Einstein, who wrote to Tesla, praising him for his "magnificent success" in his life as an inventor.[35] And if his name is familiar to you, it could be because Elon Musk named one of his companies after the scientist.

Yet Nikola Tesla did not have a promising start. As a child, he suffered from malaria as well as a whole host of other illnesses. Then he was bedridden with cholera for nine months. His condition became so serious that his family thought he would die and ordered a coffin to be made for the boy. His father, Milutin, had always wanted his son to go into the clergy, but Tesla suggested that he might recover if he were allowed to study engineering instead. No doubt, not wanting to upset the child, Milutin agreed that he would allow him to pursue his interest if he recovered. And despite his having been close to death, Tesla's health soon improved.

Things still did not go smoothly, however. Although no longer suffering with cholera, Tesla needed time to fully recover his strength. Unfortunately, he was fast approaching the age when he would have to perform his compulsory national service in the Austro-Hungarian army. And fearing that the experience would kill him, Milutin told his son to flee to the mountains. From the fall of 1874 to the summer of

1875, Tesla wandered the countryside, his only possessions a rifle and some books. In the meantime, Milutin managed to arrange a scholarship for his son at the Joanneum Polytechnic in return for eight years' military service instead of the usual three.[36] Later, Tesla worked for the Continental Edison Company in Paris and then in the United States, where he remained and later experimented on lighting, motors, and energy, announcing at the age of seventy-seven that he was on the verge of tapping a source of energy that had so far been "undreamed of" and that "was 'violently opposed' to Einsteinian physics." The energy, said Tesla, would be available everywhere.[37]

Of course, most people don't suffer an injury as dramatic or self-evident as Kahlo's or Bowie's or a childhood sickness as dramatic as Tesla's. But a hidden scar, a physical attribute ridiculed in childhood, or even a sense of being different can all be the beginnings of a journey that might take years or decades to unfold or, at least, can take us places in life that seemed unthinkable in childhood. Do not surrender to society's appeals to you to wallow in the belief that you were disadvantaged, a victim. And conversely, be cautious of the typical self-help career advice to think about the things you enjoyed doing as a child so you will supposedly know what you should do as an adult. Know what inspired and inspires you, but as we have said, reflect on the things you struggled with. Do not consider your struggles, differences, accidents, or illnesses as proof of weakness. Rather, like the tribal shaman who suffered sickness or madness and who underwent a ritual death and rebirth, see these as an initiation that opened your eyes to your inner depths and strengths.

5

The Discipline of
Positive Thinking

For all of our technological sophistication and for all the fixation on safety and convenience in the West, we have become increasingly stressed and increasingly unable to endure difficulties.[1] Yet there may be good reasons for this, for much of what sustained human cultures for tens of thousands of years has been swept away in less than a few centuries. We earlier looked at the atomization of society and the decline in membership in clubs. Consequently, the rituals of close-knit communities have more or less disappeared as well. In the West, fewer and fewer people cook, and fewer families eat meals together. Fathers do not teach their sons a trade. In cities, neighbors rarely socialize together and often do not know each other's names. People rarely attend religious services together (or even at all). And if the seasons are marked, for many people they are marked by the holiday sales.

We are trapped in our own psyches. We do what we want to do, eat what we want to eat, buy what we want to buy, and believe what we want to believe. The great metaphysical questions not only go unanswered, they also go unasked. And into the void floods politics.

Politics makes us feel moral when we attack others and intelligent when we repeat what everyone else is saying. It fires our passion and gives us a sense that, at last, there is something that we really care about. And at work or at a party, we can regurgitate the latest talking point, not only to bond with others around a shared "issue" but also to hide who we really are deep down—to hide it from others and to hide it from ourselves.

Society is happy to play this game with us. High school teachers, university professors, and political pundits—all priests of modern society—are keen for us to believe in the latest issue, to speak the same words that they speak, to signal one's conformity, and more than anything, to feel a burning anger at "the system" of which they are so obviously a part and work to sustain. Creative individuals who have developed practical solutions to the problems that the political people claim to care about are nonetheless ignored by them. What they want more than anything is not a solution but a problem. And most of all, they want a problem that can unite them, even if it is only through a sense of anger or outrage.

There is a great appeal to us to feel weak and helpless and to present ourselves as victims. It is difficult to find or to create a sense of purpose that is ours alone and to work toward it. And it is difficult to immerse ourselves in pleasure or joy. But it is easy to wallow in our own suffering, real or imagined, and to find in it a sense of purpose, righteousness, and importance, and even a sense of community. So the appeal is very strong. The human being is a herd animal. He wants to be like other people, to conform to them. But going from one job to the next (and having the threat of being laid off, demoted, or sidelined hanging over his head), gaining and losing friends, moving to new neighborhoods, having nothing permanent and communal in his life, experiencing no collective ritual, and not believing in anything transcendent, he is atomized. He is alone. In the mob, there are "substantial affective ties," notes Sigmund Freud. The mob is communal, and whether marching and chanting in unison or destroying what lies in its path, its acts are part of a ritual. And through the ritual, the atomized person is able to sink himself into the "mass individual," experiencing a momentary release of angst. For in the mob, as Freud observes, there is "a weakening of intellectual performance," an exaggeration of emotion, an "inability to exercise moderation" in expression or action.[2]

In ancient and traditional cultures and villages, it was the community—the creative collective—that exiled the individual. In modernity, however, the mob is exiled from individual greatness. Notably, a millennium ago, the "outlaw" was one who had been utterly rejected by his village, clan, or tribe. He was beneath contempt. Yet over the last half a century, the "outlaw" has been transformed into the man or woman who defies society and who has the inner strength and power to defy it.

The mob despises the individual who willingly and willfully stands outside of it in defiance of its moral posturing. Every member of the collective senses that it has—and that they have—been exiled by the outlaw, the higher individual. His presence exposes the truth of their lives: they are ordinary, dull, and predictable. The response is rage. How can it be that they, who associate themselves with the moral majority, could still be alone? The only defense of the mob is to attempt to degrade the outlaw before society, the nation, or humanity itself in the hope that they will exile and silence the individual. The government, an international corporation, the police, free speech— whatever the mob normally attacks is temporarily embraced so that it can be used against the outlaw.

Unsurprisingly, against such a background, attempting to improve one's own life, creativity, and positive thinking fall under suspicion or are frequently denounced, though not always for explicitly ideological reasons. It is certainly the case that encouragement to lift oneself up is not infrequently seen as oppressive (since there must be some people who aren't capable of it), but often positive thinking is simply misrepresented in the media as wishful thinking or self-delusion. And certainly, it isn't difficult to come across people who pepper every conversation with positive-thinking clichés while merely floating through life, never committing to what they say they really want to do (and have the time, money, and opportunity to do). Most people just want a little hope, an easy life, and to feel a little bit special, after all.

However, tempering one's thoughts, having hope, and finding the good is not a new approach to life. Religions, which have generally grasped that life is brutal and unfair, have encouraged their disciples to foster this attitude. Hope is one of the three theological virtues of the Catholic Church (the other two being faith and charity or love). In the Quran (Surah al-Baqarah 2:152), the believer is instructed not to be ungrateful. "With chanting praises I present all good thoughts, good words, and good deeds," reads the ancient Persian sacred text, the Zend-Avesta, "and with rejection I repudiate all evil thoughts, and words, and deeds."[3] Likewise, the classic text of Buddhist thought, the Dhammapada, opens with the following four stanzas:

All that we are is the result of what we have thought: it is founded on our thoughts, it is made up of our thoughts. If a man speaks or acts with an evil thought, pain follows him, as the wheel follows the foot of the ox that draws the carriage.

All that we are is the result of what we have thought: it is founded on our thoughts, it is made up of our thoughts. If a man speaks or acts with a pure thought, happiness follows him, like a shadow that never leaves him.

"He abused me, he beat me, he defeated me, he robbed me,"—in those who harbour such thoughts hatred will never cease.

"He abused me, he beat me, he defeated me, he robbed me,"—in those who do not harbour such thoughts hatred will cease.[4]

Traditionally considered to be the words of the Buddha himself, these words are as relevant today as in the millennia past. Containing the thoughts and focusing on the good is a discipline as challenging as any other. Moreover, mental discipline is integral to martial arts, weight lifting, and athletics, among other pursuits. As we have already mentioned, legendary boxing trainer Cus D'Amato introduced Mike Tyson to the positive thinking practice of Émile Coué during his early training.[5] For those such as D'Amato, positive thinking is part of the necessary work of disciplining the mind and not letting it surrender to negativity and fear. For others, it is about escaping poverty or illness or having to face challenges that would test anyone. It is not easy. It is not about rainbows, unicorns, and a comfortable life. It is about mental fighting. I encourage you to cultivate a practice of positive thinking, not because life is easy but precisely because it is hard—not to fool yourself, but to arm yourself for the struggles ahead.

Coué visited the United States during the 1920s, and his method caught on, eventually becoming a positive-thinking cliché.[6] Every morning and evening, the individual would quietly repeat to himself, twenty times, "Every day, in every way, I am getting better and better." Often, more specific statements are said or thought to oneself. In his booklet *It Works,* published in 1926, R. H. Jarrett instructed readers to make a list of the things that they really want in their life and to read it morning, noon, and night. He also suggested that the individual should think about what he wanted as often as possible, though he should not tell anyone about it. Instead, Jarrett suggested, he should speak about it only to the "Great Power" or God. Whether the practitioner believes in God, gods and goddesses, a Higher Power, Higher Self, or Higher Consciousness, the sense that he or she is communicating with an intelligence that transcends and lies outside of his or her own consciousness is important.

Adding to positive thinking, the author and minister Norman Vincent Peale advocated "positive imaging" (visualizing one's desires). He, too, suggested that this practice should be "combined with a strong religious faith" as well as with prayer and the giving of thanks, as if one's desires had already been fulfilled.[7] Peale tells us that the individual must consciously visualize his or her desire or goal "with tremendous intensity, reinforced by prayer." Doing this, he says, will make the unconscious accept it and "activate it."[8] To make the unconscious—or subconscious—accept the goal more easily, some practitioners will visualize it while they are in a light trance state, most especially in the hypnagogic state, when your mind and body are very relaxed and you are about to drift off to sleep, or in the hypnopompic state, when you are waking up from sleep but have not yet regained full waking consciousness.

What sort of thing should you focus on? Author Mitch Horowitz says that "it's not about daydreams or fantasies but attainable concrete goals."[9] Ask yourself not only what you want to achieve but also what you can achieve if you put enough effort into it. In other words, ask what you are driven to achieve. Huge goals can be incapacitating. They can seem unattainable. Instead, set high but reasonable goals. If you think it is possible to achieve a huge goal, break it down. Mark Divine (commander, U.S. Navy SEALS, retired) gives us several techniques for battling through a challenging situation that will be applicable here: visualization (which we have already mentioned), goal setting, self-talk, and deep breathing.[10]

Involving deep breathing and concentration, when it is used properly, trance is a meditative technique for becoming more conscious of our higher nature or Higher Self and aligning ours thoughts and actions to it. If you do not have a clear idea of how you want to live, consider what kind of work you want to do, how close to or far from nature you want to live, what kind of food you want to eat, what kind of friends you want to have, how close you will be to your family, the kind of aesthetics you want to be surrounded by (e.g., what you want your home, city, or village to look like; what kind of clothes you want to wear; what you want your body to look like), and so on. This will give you some kind of picture of where you want to go. And you will probably be able to make small changes in several areas of your life immediately.

Goal setting is about taking manageable risks that, if they work out, will be of real benefit to you and will get you closer to your aim but that will not create overwhelming or unmanageable negative consequences in your life if they do not. Such risks help us to get where we want to go by breaking the journey to it into steps. Let's take an example from physical training. If you want to do a hundred push-ups, you might break them into sets of ten. And even if you do a hundred straight, you still might want to focus on ten at a time. (Psychologically, if a hundred seems too much of a challenge, focusing only on ten at a time until you reach a hundred might not. You, after all, will get to see your successes as you work through the set. You have done ten, twenty, thirty, or more, so what is another ten?) Again, if you want to paint a large oil painting, you can break it down into drawing the layout, laying down flat color over the drawing, then painting successive layers for dimension and detail. When it comes to goal setting, consider whether you are really making use of all of your assets, especially time. Ask yourself whether you are spending some time unwisely each day, perhaps wasting an hour or so in the morning as you dread going to work or in the evening when unwinding from your day job. That would not be unusual.

We will look at fear later on, but here we should note that self-talk helps us to face situations that we find challenging or fearful. It is simply the technique of countering negative thoughts such as *I can't do this* with *I can do this* or thoughts such as *you're a failure* with *you're going to be a success*. Self-talk is useful when we have committed to a course of action and are approaching our first challenge. You must have prepared yourself for the situation and know that you are prepared and can prevail. Self-talk is not self-delusion or wishful thinking. You must prepare, knowing as much as possible about what you are walking into and having taken all the necessary steps for success beforehand. If your task requires physical training, then you must train physically. If it requires acquiring a skill or learning something new, then you must acquire that skill or knowledge and understanding. Self-talk is not a shortcut.

Deep breathing helps to calm the individual, enabling him to regain control of his thoughts and emotions. In general, people breathe only into their chests, while those who meditate sometimes breathe only into their stomachs. While there are different techniques, deep breathing means, simply, breathing into both the chest and stomach so that both inflate with the inhalation and deflate with the exhalation. You do not need to be in a stressful situation to breathe deeply. Simply become conscious of your breathing, breathe slowly and relaxed, inflating the chest and stomach as you breathe in and deflating them as you breathe out. Do not force the breath or strain the lungs. This will only increase tension emotionally and in your body.

Sticking with our example of physical exercise, if you haven't worked out for two decades and are out of shape, becoming a champion bodybuilder might be impossible, at least right now. Even if that's your dream, set one of your goals as losing a reasonable amount of weight or gaining a certain amount of muscle over the next six months. Write this down on your list. Clearly visualize how you are going to look. Visualize it when you wake up in the morning or at some other time of day. But take action as well. Get your doctor to check you out and make sure you're fit enough for a new regimen of physical training. And then get a trainer or join a gym, and work out on a regular basis. Make it part of your routine. And make appropriate changes to your diet that will help you lose excess fat or gain some weight if you are underweight, gain muscle, and get healthier. Once you've achieved your goal for the next six months or year, you can build on that.

Whatever it is that you want to achieve, build working toward it into your routine. Perhaps you're a night person and can work when everyone else in your home has gone to sleep. If so, do that. Or perhaps evenings are too busy and you're more of a morning person, or you lie in bed for an hour before getting up, dreading the day ahead. If so, get up early and work on your goal for that hour. Don't be disheartened by the thought of doing small amounts at a time. You will be headed in the right direction. And it will eventually add up.

Let's return to physical exercise again for a moment. Many people don't work out because they believe that this will mean going to the gym for a two-hour session at least once a week—and they don't have that time. (Be aware that many people won't compromise with their alleged ideal precisely to give themselves an excuse to do nothing.) What about working out for ten minutes a day? (They do have that amount of time to spare.) How many push-ups, sit-ups, or squats can be done in a solid ten minutes? A lot. It's not enough to become a champion bodybuilder, but it's infinitely superior to no exercise at all, ever. And it's a foundation to build on. Once you get momentum, you will find ways to do more. But if you never start, you won't.

Although we've used physical exercise as an example, I encourage you to develop yourself mentally, physically, and spiritually. Perhaps you want to learn a new subject or read more often, get stronger, practice a martial art, improve your posture, cook better food, dress a little better, or meditate more often. You will probably be able to integrate some of your aims into your daily life. Others you will need to dedicate specific time to. Before you go to bed, know what you will work on tomorrow. As you wake up, visualize yourself having achieved your goals and desires. Create a plan, make it simple enough to remember, and get into the habit of doing it.

However, once you get into a routine, do not fall into the trap of doing the work in a daydream. Do it with full attention. Make your self-development work into a ritual—an act of devotion to your Higher or future Self. To develop yourself mentally, physically, and spiritually, work out for thirty minutes or an hour, meditate for ten minutes or so, and then read a page or a passage of a book and sit quietly and contemplate it. Choose a classic or ancient work: the Dhammapada, the Bhagavad Gita, The Analects of Confucius, the "Hávamál" of *The Poetic Edda,* Proverbs from the Bible, *The Art of War, Hagakure,* or perhaps *The Book of Five Rings.*

6

DEVELOPING A
POWERFUL SELF-IMAGE

"WHEN YOU CHANGE A MAN'S FACE, you almost invariably change his future," claimed Maxwell Maltz, the cosmetic surgeon and author of *Psycho-Cybernetics*. Our self-image largely determines how we act in life, and how we act largely determines what paths we take in life and what we will become. (We have already mentioned David Bowie's career, which was shaped, in part, by his unusual appearance.) And yet, whether we like it or not, our self-image is inextricably linked to our body, and of all the parts of our body, it is especially linked to our face.

In his practice, Maltz had seen dramatic, positive changes in the personalities and behaviors of his patients after he had improved their looks in some way. But Maltz also noticed that surgery did not work for everyone, at least not psychologically. An individual might be attractive except for a large lump on his face, for example, and yet, even after its removal, the patient would still insist on seeing himself as ugly. It was as if the lump were still there in his own self-image, or as Maltz said, it was as if the personality itself "had a 'face.'"[1] We'll return to the self-image and how it can affect the future in a moment. But first, let's consider the face a little more.

We tend to think of facial expressions as universal. We can find smiling, laughter, and crying in every culture across the globe, after all, and we tend to laugh when we find something funny and cry when we feel sad. However, although some emotions, such as fear and disgust, are expressed through extremely similar facial expressions throughout the world, even these expressions can be subtly different and are expressed more or less often from one culture to the next.[2] To put it bluntly, people from different countries, cultures, and even classes use their facial muscles differently. This means that a person of Indian or Chinese heritage who has grown up in the West will likely be recognized as an outsider if he visits India or China, even if he dresses like everyone else when he arrives. He will use his facial muscles differently (and hold his body differently as well). And in cases of those who are older, their faces may be lined in ways or to a degree that is not typical in the country they are visiting.

Studies carried out by psychologist Paula Marie Niedenthal and a number of her graduate students at the University of Wisconsin have shown that there is a good reason for the difference in facial expressions. In countries with a history of higher migration over the last five hundred years (such as Canada and the United States), people tend to be more expressive with their facial gestures and smile more, whereas in countries with historically very low levels of migration (such as China and Japan), people tend to be less expressive in their facial gestures and smile less. Moreover, in the countries that had experienced more migration, smiling was associated with friendliness, while in the more ethnically, racially, and culturally homogenous countries, smiling was viewed as a way of demonstrating superiority.[3]

Perhaps the increased use of facial expressions—and of smiling in particular—was meant to help overcome the language barriers between people of different backgrounds and to help them communicate, at least on a basic level.[4] Or perhaps in more homogenous cultures with uniform manners, language, and greater physical similarity, only subtle gestures are needed to express an emotion or a view, especially dissent from the norm; hence, the stoic and unemotional appearance of the upper-class English and the upper-class Japanese, at least traditionally.

With all of this in mind, there is something especially interesting about the appearance of the knight or the warrior. Unlike the craftsman or the priest in most cultures, the warrior often masks his face in some way, whether that is through the use of a helmet and visor, war paint, modern camouflage paint, or, to a lesser extent, the balaclava (usually associated either with special forces, such as the British Special Air Service [SAS], or with terrorist groups). It is true, of course, that the knight's helmet and visor protected the head and face of the warrior in battle. It had an obvious and practical function. But there was another aspect to the warrior's covering his head and face, an aspect that we might call psychological or even magical. He took on the personality of the helmet, mask, or paint and discarded his own.

In battle, dressed in his uniform, he became someone else. Notably, some coverings, such as the Ribchester and Crosby Garrett helmets (both found in England, though of Roman origin), were made to resemble a human head and face. The samurai appear to have understood the psychological aspect much more clearly. Their helmets often included a *men-yoroi* (face armor or visor) that featured a demonic-looking face with a grossly exaggerated expression of wrath or madness.

Other warriors associated their power with animals. Among the Norse, the berserker wore the skin of a bear and the *úlfhéðnar* the skin of a wolf. Before battle, the berserkers entered into some kind of trance state, becoming frenzied, howling like animals, and biting their shields. During battle, it was believed, the berserkers were unable to feel pain. Among the Roman legions was the *aquilifer*, a soldier who carried the legion's standard into battle. He wore a lion's skin, with its head fixed over his helmet. Jaguar warriors and eagle warriors were the highest ranks among the Aztec military. The former wore a jaguar skin over his head and back, and the latter wore a helmet shaped like an eagle's head and beak.

"Man is least himself when he talks in his own person," Oscar Wilde commented in his *Intentions*. "Give him a mask, and he will tell you the truth."[5] But as probably every premodern culture knew, if you give a man a mask, the mask will speak. Hence, dressed as a bear, the berserker, in a trance, became a bear; hence, too, the extensive use of masks in premodern societies, from the ritual tribal masks of Africa to the masks of the Japanese Noh theater. Or the wearing of a uniform, a gentleman's suit in the contemporary era, or even a certain brand of clothing (which conjures up specific associations in the mind) or the dress of a subculture. Yet there is much truth to Wilde's claim. Given anonymity and enough incentive (or sometimes given a shot at fame), an individual will say things he would normally keep secret. But as Wilde implies, our face is no less a kind of mask.

The word *person* derives from the Latin word *persona,* which originally referred to the theatrical mask worn by actors in the Roman theater.[6] We have learned to use our face—and our persona—not only to express our emotions but also to hide them and, in many circumstances, to hide our intentions as well. Hiding our true feelings and intentions begins early on, of course. In England, traditionally, mothers would tell their small children not to make an ugly or stupid face or to show displeasure or emotional upset because, they suggested, the wind would change and—for reasons unknown to us—their child's face would remain permanently like that.

"At fifty," wrote George Orwell in his diary shortly before he died, "every man has the face he deserves."[7] He may deserve it, of course, but is it really his face? Does it really express who he is? Take a look around any city, at people walking along the street or sitting on a subway train, perhaps, and you will not see the peaceful, natural face of the human being (which we might find in a village in a remote part of the world where people are still connected to the rhythms of nature), but faces full of tension, held in a default expression—often one of worry or concern. It is as if they are in a conversation yet unable to speak, as if they are being continually spoken to, and perhaps even reprimanded. Most people are unable to control their thoughts, and sooner or later, it shows on their faces.

One of the lesser-known pioneers of psychotherapy, Wilhelm Reich, noticed something similar. He believed that psychological complexes were essentially fixed and stored not solely in the psyche but also in the "muscular armour" of the body.[8] In all of the cases he had encountered, psychologically damaged individuals had suppressed feelings of hate, anger, love, and so on as children by holding their breath, tensing their stomach, or by other similar, instinctive methods.

Tension and muscular "knots" in the upper back, around the shoulder, and even in the face are common signs of long-term stress, as are clenching the jaw tight, squinting, frowning, tightening the lips, and (while seated) a continual, jittery rocking back and forth of one of the legs. Much of this is done unconsciously. But let's look at the "fight-or-flight" response to a threat. This, too, involves the body: Breathing becomes deeper to fill the body with oxygen and energy so that it can respond quickly. Blood flow is reduced to the skin and increased to the muscles. The muscles might tremble. The pupils will dilate. Nothing in this response is conscious.

Over time, our anxiety becomes fixed in the physical body, rigidifying part of it. Yet, as Reich noted, psychologists have concerned themselves only with what thoughts or emotions the individual was trying to suppress and why he was trying to suppress them. If the physical tension itself could be loosened, claimed Reich, it would not only release the natural physical energy of the body but would also stimulate the individual to recall a "memory" of the traumatic event that caused him to begin tensing in a particular way in the first place. The psychologist had to work on the body as much as the mind. "The psychic structure" (meaning the psychological structure), Reich said, "is at the same time a biophysiological structure."[9]

"The flow of our spiritual energy controls the body, and all things that enter the spirit do, in time, have an effect on the body," says Don Lambert in *Kung Fu Wu Su: A Memoir,* and they will "show up in our eyes, our faces, and our mannerisms."[10] It should be clear by now that to get control of ourselves and to begin to get control of our destinies, we have to work on the body and not just on the thinking. And this partly means learning to relax. We should not confuse tension for strength, toughness, or seriousness. Even the harder styles of martial arts require much more relaxation than people generally realize. When a martial artist punches, he does not tense his arm the entire time. The fist is tight, but the arm is relaxed until an inch or so before it connects with the target. Relaxation gives the punch more speed, and more speed means more power. And relaxation gives us power in many different situations. If we are relaxed, then we are usually more confident than when we are tense, and being relaxed, we are able to adapt to circumstances much more easily.

You must begin to perceive the levels of tension and relaxation in your own body and must begin to balance them in a way that is natural. Let's consider meditation briefly. Often, when a person begins to learn to meditate, he will become so relaxed that he begins to slouch. His torso might even appear to completely collapse. He will have relaxed to a point of almost falling asleep. Like the martial artist, the meditator needs to retain a certain amount of tension (i.e., enough to keep the correct posture). And this, of course, applies to daily life. We want to be relaxed without sacrificing our posture or mental alertness.

There is an easy way to begin to do this. Stand with the feet apart so that they are more or less parallel to your shoulders. Let your arms hang loose by your sides, but pull the shoulders back a little so that you are not slouching. Bend your knees slightly. Relax, and breathe slowly in for a moment. Be conscious of your breathing. Focus on the inhalation and exhalation, but remain relaxed. Now imagine that there is a hook in the center of the top of your head and that you are being pulled up slightly by that hook. Do not feel tense, and do not lock the knees. Allow this visualization to align your body: lift the head so that your jaw is parallel to the ground, balance your head on your neck, and raise your diaphragm. Remain in this posture for a few moments, concentrating on your breathing and remaining relaxed. Meditation can be performed standing as well as sitting. And this, in effect, is what you are doing.

However, just as Miyamoto Musashi advised samurai warriors to make their fighting posture their ordinary posture, so you must be able to retain an upright, confident posture while being relaxed and open during the day, especially when speaking or engaging with other people.[11] And you must be able to retain a good posture whether you are standing, sitting, or reclining. To be able to do that, you will need to be conscious of your posture and your level of relaxation, making adjustments when you notice that you are slouching or too stiff, too relaxed, or too tense.

We are not just working on the body; we also are working on the persona. And there are two major psychological issues that we can face in regard to the persona.[12] We might identify too strongly with our employment, career status, social position, or some role that we might have to perform as part of our life and interactions with other people.[13] We might think of ourselves as a lawyer, manager, doctor, artist, father, son, Republican, or Democrat, taking pride in our identity (or identities) and seeing ourselves as intellectually or morally superior, for example. Yet we might be completely unaware of our real interests or values. Conversely, we might suffer from a lack of persona. Such a person does not, of course, identify himself with his roles in society. However, this is partly because he may be barely able to represent himself to other people, speaking too softly to be heard, refusing to look other people in the eyes, and allowing himself to be taken advantage of. He might slouch or seem disengaged and directionless. He has no apparent ambition. No drive or desire.

Jungian-oriented psychotherapist and author Robert H. Hopcke has identified three major steps to developing an authentic persona. First, an individual should become conscious of his persona as it currently is and should understand how and why it functions and, of course, where he is using it to really represent himself and where he is using it to hide himself. Here, we have added another task or technique: he must learn to relax, to feel the tension in his body that has built up over a number of years, and to become aware of how he stresses and strains his body and how he uses his face or how certain inauthentic expressions come automatically at times of embarrassment or anxiety. And he must learn to give up those mechanisms.

Second, says Hopcke, the individual should then begin to develop a more authentic persona. And third, he should begin interacting in the world with this "more functional persona."[14] To begin to develop a more authentic persona, the individual should ask himself who he is, what he stands for, and what are his values and beliefs. He must develop self-awareness if he is to forge a new self-image. When he has a clearer idea, he can begin to ask himself how he can express his true Self and what might be the most effective and powerful ways of communicating his real values and convictions to others and to the world around him.[15]

Here, we are touching on positive thinking or positive imaging again. As we have seen, in its most basic form, the practice of positive thinking requires the individual to carve out a clear image of what he wants in life, to recall it every day, perhaps visualizing it, and to diligently and intelligently pursue it.

The reason positive thinking often fails, Maltz claimed, is that so many people are unable or unwilling to change their self-image or persona. If an individual dreams of being an artist yet, upon producing one inferior work, starts thinking of himself as not artistic or as a failure in the art world, he will not be able to succeed in it. Someone might have the ambition to learn a martial art yet quit after a single tough workout or upon being beaten, the first time he spars, by a more advanced student. This defeatism starts early in life. A child fails a test and instead of saying, "I failed that test," he says, "I am a failure." He identifies himself with the failure and tells himself that he cannot learn this subject or will never be good at some other thing.[16] He becomes the person who cannot do, or who cannot achieve, or, perhaps especially as an adult, who cannot be happy.

Why do we form an inauthentic persona in the first place? Insecurity and a desire to fit in might be two reasons. Past trauma might be another. In our own pasts, we have all suffered embarrassment, shame, loss, belittlement, feelings of powerlessness, and feelings of being weak or ugly. No matter how much a person grows, sometimes he feels anchored to a past trauma.

As Maltz points out, the self-image is changed only through "experiencing."[17] Yet we can "experience" to a degree through visualization. Try the following: Sit or lie down, relax, and breathe slowly and deeply. Begin to recall an episode of mild shame or embarrassment, not as if it's happening to you, but from the perspective of someone watching from the outside. If you suffered bullying, for example, recall it, but having remembered it, change what you imagine. Don't see yourself as the victim. Instead, visualize yourself calmly telling the victimizer why he is wrong and why he is acting out of his own weakness and telling him to stop. Imagine yourself standing, acting, and speaking confidently, as you would now. Imagine that you are saying this to help him. And imagine him realizing that he has done wrong and not proceeding with his past behavior.

Or if you felt ugly at some part in your life, again, recall this, but then imagine standing confidently, relaxed, and smiling. Imagine wearing different and better clothing, if you want to, or with a different haircut, or with a body improved through a healthy diet and exercise. See yourself acting then as you would act now or want to act now. See yourself as strong, confident, well liked, and concerned with the well-being of others.

We have to take action in the present, however. Because we are also considering the biophysiological structure, we can add to these second and third steps that the individual should begin to develop a new posture—upright, relaxed, and adaptable—and a new sense of his face and of his self. Aim to become conscious of your posture and facial expression in different situations. Let's try some simple techniques, starting with the face:

Lie down, and relax. Breathe deeply for a moment or two. Then, with the fingertips of both hands, press gently across your forehead, feeling for any tension. Then do the same between, across, and very slightly above your eyebrows. Then press gently on either side of your nose, below your eye sockets. Then work your way across your jaw. Then press below your ears, where your jaw meets your neck. Move the jaw up and down slowly as you do this. Last, starting near the neck, press your thumbs gently under your jaw, behind the jawbone. You will probably have found quite a lot of tension in some of those areas. If so, go back, and gently massage those areas, relieving the tension.

Now relax, and become conscious of your face. Begin at the forehead, and work down through the face to the jaw, mentally, observing any tension at all. If you feel tension somewhere, relax that area. If you feel your face is totally relaxed, mentally work through it again from top to bottom, observing any other tension that you detect. Most likely, you will be able to detect several layers of tension. Do this exercise every day, and if possible, at the moment of waking up, before you are fully conscious, tell yourself to relax your face. You will probably find that there is already some tension.

You can also start from the bottom of the face. Try the following: With the mentalis muscle (center of the chin), pull the chin down for a few seconds. Then become conscious of the lips and the muscles around the mouth, and tense them very slightly, as if you are about to smile (but do not smile or move the lips). Then relax beneath the eyes. Relax the eyelids. And relax the brow and forehead. Last, imagine a diagonal line from the left corner of your mouth to the outside corner of your left eye and another diagonal line from the right corner of the mouth to the outside corner of your right eye. Imagine that you are about to smile, not just with your mouth but also with the muscles along those lines.

A martial artist will practice a punch, kick, or block thousands of times. His aim is to commit it to muscle memory so that he does not need to think about or remember the technique consciously to be able to perform it. Problematically for us, we commit our stresses, tension, fears, and negative thoughts to the muscle memory of our faces. In the above exercise, however, we began to undo that. Our aim is not solely to be able to relax our facial muscles. We also want to be able to let go of yesterday's tension, stress, and automatic facial responses so that we do not become overwhelmed by defeatist thoughts that have become subconscious. As an illustration, if you do a simple exercise such as push-ups, try this: When you have reached the point where you are straining, feeling some pain or weakness in the muscles and are beginning to grimace, to push yourself through the experience, relax your face instead. Notice that once you do this, it becomes more evident that the pain is located only in your arms. This feels much more manageable. Notice, too, that even when you take a shower, you might make different expressions in response to water running down your face.

We want to align what Maltz considered the personality of the face more closely with our true nature. Become aware of your facial expressions, especially when interacting with other people. Do you habitually squint, widen your eyes, screw up your face, frown, smile, or stare at the floor when someone makes you nervous? If so, when you are alone and relaxed, try to do the opposite. If you squint or make your eyes wider than natural when nervous, relax them. If you frown, relax the forehead. If you clench your jaw, relax your jaw and relax your chin. However, understand that tension in one area of the face might affect another, so always take the whole face into consideration, and see whether the tension you feel being caused by tension somewhere else in the face that you were not aware of.

Last, once you are able to relax your face and have become conscious of your habitual facial expressions, begin to think about your natural face. The Zen Buddhist monk Myo once asked the Sixth Patriarch to explain Zen to him. The patriarch responded by saying to not dwell on that duality of good and evil and asking, "What is your original face before you were born?"[18] Think about the face of the monk, the confident leader, or the man peacefully absorbed in his work. And think about your original face. Now let's move on to the body.

To begin to understand your posture, go out for a walk and mentally observe your body. Perhaps you tend to walk with your shoulders hunched and head down or with your body stiff and robotic. Although it is likely that your posture dictates the speed at which you walk, conversely, your speed of walking affects your posture. It is difficult to walk fast while hunching the shoulders and staring at the ground, lost in thought, and it is difficult to be stiff and robotic while walking slowly. So vary your speed, and see how this affects your posture and how that affects your sense of self. If you tend to walk fast, slow down and relax the body. If you tend to walk slowly, walk quicker. Observe your body, too, when you are standing or sitting. Do you slouch? Do you nervously face slightly away from the person you are talking to? Is your body too tense? Remember to stand relaxed but upright, as if you are being pulled up by a hook at the center of your head.

Last, let's look at clothing. In *The Law of Success,* Napoleon Hill describes how he spent a great deal of money on three hand-tailored suits. Then he went for a walk each morning, along a certain street where he knew he would pass by a wealthy publisher. Hill made sure to speak to the publisher each morning. Then, after a week, he decided to say nothing, to see if the publisher would speak to him. As Hill walked by, the publisher stopped him and commented on his clothes, saying he looked "damn prosperous," and inquired about his line of work. Hill said he was about to launch a magazine. Unsurprisingly, the publisher reminded Hill that that was his profession and invited him to his club, where he offered to finance the magazine.[19]

Perhaps Hill's approach was not entirely ethical, but his point was simple. Just as Maltz believed the face has a personality, Hill believed that there is a "psychology of clothes."[20] Your clothing will have an effect on those whom you meet and engage with, and more importantly, it will affect you and, for better or worse, will help shape your self-image. And for Hill, his tailored suits gave him the feeling of being a man of "self-reliance" that he needed if he was going to pursue his lost fortune.[21]

One thing you need to be aware of, however, is that people often think about their own clothing symbolically. A woman will wear an ill-fitting black or red dress and a man will wear an ill-fitting, cheaply made suit, believing that the dress or the suit will "make a statement" about the wearer (e.g., by simply wearing a suit, an individual might believe he is signaling a level of financial success or that he is a professional or an adult). It is a mistake to think about clothing in this way. Your aim is not to get your clothing noticed by others; it is to get you noticed. When other people see you, they should be intrigued by you, not by your clothing. Wear what fits and what suits you, not what "symbolizes" you or "makes a statement."

7

FEAR AND THE
HIGHER SELF

FEAR. It is obvious that men do not fear those small things that they can easily contend with, but rather fear things that seem too great and too strange to triumph over. We fear what can defeat us, destroy us, or take away all we have, including our sense of who we are. There have, of course, always been plenty of things to fear—war, tyrannical leaders, violent oppression, disease, famine, robbery, murder, and so on—but throughout the history of mankind, fear was kept in check by faith.

Ancient man believed that he was a participant in a cosmic drama and would go to Valhalla, the hall of the gods, if he died in battle. Or he believed that God would protect him or that, no matter what, everything that happened to him was the Will of God. And that he would be rewarded in the afterlife for his faith. Or at the very least, he believed in the monarch or in the military leader whom he would fight with or for, seeing that person as chosen by the gods or by God. In the premodern world, to express fear was to expose oneself as someone who lacked faith in the God who had created everything and who sustained everything.

Today, however, we are confident that modern man has—or should have—all the answers and all the technical sophistication to solve every imaginable problem, whether global, national, social, political, biological, technological, or psychological. Inevitably, in such a human-centric world, faith strikes us as old fashioned and unsophisticated. Yet as we have demoted faith and God and have elevated man, we have also unwittingly elevated fear. Fear, as sociologist and author Frank Furedi has noted, "increasingly serves as a metaphor for interpreting life."[1] It has, in effect, taken over the role of faith.

The modern world offers us no sense that there is anything permanent and no sense of being connected to the sacred. There is a great churning momentum. Everything is in a state of flux, fleeting, and breaking apart. The very things that give our lives meaning—friendships, relationships, marriage, jobs, careers—can all suddenly end, and often do. In the premodern world, God watched over the man who went into the desert or the forest. The hermit spoke to Him and saw in nature signs that He had answered. In a city of millions of people, we are alone.

We want to "escape from the agony called insecurity."[2] We feel the anxiety of a million little things in our own lives, worrying that we made a mistake at work, that our romantic partner might leave us, that we don't have enough money saved, or that we can't afford a visit to the doctor. We want to be free of this gnawing fear the way that the nicotine addict wants to be rid of the withdrawal. And we crave another type of fear—a social, human-centric type of fear—in the way that the chain-smoker craves another cigarette, or perhaps the way that an individual might crave the fear of the horror movie or the roller-coaster ride.

This fear makes us feel right—morally right, even. It gives us a sense of certainty. We know what we should fear and what we should not. We do not have to fear nature or God. We do not even truly fear the hurricane, flood, or virus. Rather, we fear that the politicians, doctors, scientists, and NGOs will not act quickly enough to save us from the hurricane, flood, or virus. No matter how incompetent people seem to be in practice, we are convinced that nothing is beyond the control of the cleverest human minds (whom we are clever enough to recognize and to agree with).

We agree with the actions of the governor, mayor, or president, no matter how adversely they affect people who live in a different part of town or different part of the country or who have a very different financial situation because we fear what will happen to us if they don't act. We denounce our political opponents, claiming they are motivated by fear (which makes them irrational and immoral) and that, for precisely that reason, we need to fear them. To put it more succinctly, our opponents' fear delegitimizes their claims whereas our fear legitimizes ours. This type of fear masks the insecurity and anxiety we feel about our own actions and our own lives with a sense of certainty, moral superiority, and—since we feel bonded to those who share our fears—even a sense of community.

Yet life is a thinly disguised chaos. And no matter how much we would like to believe otherwise, on both a small and a large scale, things turn out differently from what we expect or hope for, and different even from what we fear. Even on a personal level, we experience the unexpected: Plans are broken. Sickness, death, misfortune, or financial hardship invades our life. We experience sudden, unexpected violence. We become the subject of gossip, are falsely accused, and find our kindness repaid with unkindness.

"Begin the morning by saying to thyself, I shall meet with the busybody, the ungrateful, arrogant, deceitful, envious, unsocial," advised

Marcus Aurelius.[3] More than one-and-a-half millennia later, in one of his most famous poems, "If," Rudyard Kipling talks of the unfairness of life and how we should respond to it. We might, Kipling tells us, find people lying about us, hating us, losing their heads, and blaming us. Our words might be twisted. We might lose all we have. And we will meet with the "two imposters": Triumph and Disaster. Yet through it all, Kipling advises us, we should cultivate what might be called "non-attachment." If other people are losing their heads, we should not lose ours. If someone hates us, we should not respond by hating him. If someone lies about us, we should not respond by lying. If we lose everything we have, we should not complain but should begin again.

Today, estranged from nature and with a "belief" in science and faith in politics, many people in the West find it almost impossible to accept that life is inherently chaotic, unsafe, and often unfair, or that brutality can invade it at any time, or that we will be treated unjustly at times and in ways both large and small. Yet no matter how much we might deny it, we can be afflicted by misfortune, loss, and suffering at any moment, without warning. We have all experienced it. And as we saw earlier, so many successful, famous, and influential people have had to wrestle against serious adversity—serious childhood illnesses, serious accidents, poverty, or a learning disability.

If we are working toward discovering our true Self or our Higher Self and trying to embody our higher nature or higher ideals, what are setbacks, losses, defeats, tragedies, and difficult times for? Or at least, what should be our attitude toward them? Such misfortunes, after all, can lead to real suffering, perhaps financial and certainly mental and emotional. We might feel that there is something wrong with us, and we might be tempted to punish or hurt ourselves in some way, drowning ourselves in drink or drugs or acting aggressively to those few who still support us in a perverse attempt to push them away, to save them from us. Or conversely, we might be tempted to blame other people.

But often, when enough time passes, we can look back and acknowledge that what we were hoping for was the easy road or a comfortable safety net. That is understandable. Some people do have—or appear to have—an easy life. And in an unpredictable world, there are good reasons to want that—very good reasons. But here, we are asking, what should our attitude be in the face of misfortune? (Or in the face of what, at the time, we perceive as misfortune?) First, we must acknowledge that while no one is unhappy to experience "good luck," good fortune early on often translates into misfortune later in life. People get comfortable with not having to try and eventually become afraid of pushing themselves, even to get the things that they might truly want. They can stagnate and become resentful, even though they may have material comfort. Even with luxury all around them, they can feel unfulfilled and unhappy. Conversely, a tough life early on has, as we have seen, often been an incentive for an individual to push himself far beyond his peers and to forge his own path in life, one that uniquely reflects who he is.

"Patience," says the Dhammapada, is the highest practice.[4] Patience is necessary. Persistence is key. Through encountering trials and tribulations and persisting, we develop character, inner strength, insight, knowledge, and perhaps some wisdom. Sooner or later, opportunities open up as well, and we begin to find a path through life, whether winding or straight. Yet even then, we are likely to find ourselves facing significant threats to our well-being, and we will continue to face significant obstacles and challenges. Having become probably Rome's greatest military leader of the day, Julius Caesar was afflicted by either epilepsy or ministrokes, and not long before becoming emperor, at the battle of Thapsus in 46 BCE, he collapsed from this condition and had to be taken to safety.[5] We are highly unlikely to reach a point where we are perfectly safe from the whims of Fate.

"Fear of the Lord is the beginning of wisdom," says Proverbs 9:10. But why fear God—a God who is love, in particular—when there is so much else to fear? There has been great confusion about this statement in the Bible. To the modern individual, living in comfort, it seems to represent the religion of "fire and brimstone" of earlier, ignorant ages. It seems to say that we should live in fear of religious authority. But Proverbs does not say that fear of the priest or the minister is the beginning of wisdom. Nor fear of our neighbors, our enemies, or natural disasters, or sickness or death. Rather, it says that fear of God, or the Lord, "is the beginning of wisdom."

Fearing "the Lord," the individual does not fear man. Or perhaps anything else. He fears—has chosen to fear—what is bigger than everything else combined: friend, enemy, hurricane, sickness, and death. We know, of course, that, like politics, religion can be, and has been, used as an excuse to look down on, and even to hate, people with different beliefs. But if someone truly meditates on God—not religion, but God—then the ego cannot stand up to Him. Hence, one ancient Greek myth tells us that when the god Zeus showed the priestess Semele a mere glimpse of his true glory, from which emerged thunderbolts and storm clouds, she was instantly destroyed.

In Ezekiel, too, the Biblical prophet sees a cloud of fire in the sky (Ezekiel 1:4), followed by the appearance of a creature with the face of a man, a lion, an ox, and an eagle (Ezekiel 1:10). Finally, seated on a throne, the Biblical prophet beholds Yahweh, whose body is like fire (Ezekiel 1:26–27). Yahweh instructs Ezekiel to go to the "children of Israel," since they have rebelled against God. And he tells the prophet not to be afraid of the people there or afraid of their words, even "though briers and thorns be with thee, and thou dost dwell among scorpions" (Ezekiel 2:6). Instead, says Yahweh, Ezekiel will speak the words of God to them (Ezekiel 2:7).

The Lord is the ultimate danger. He is both more distant and closer than any disaster that could befall us. He is the Creator who is somehow apart from this world and who gives us the space to exist within it and to explore—to seek God, to seek out that ultimate danger, and within it, to come face-to-face with ourselves. And He is also our conscience, our sense of guilt at doing the wrong thing or not being true to ourselves or our word; and He is our will, our vision, and our determination to push on against the odds and despite the obstacles to our destiny.

The searching man seeks out dangerous spaces—the mountain, the dojo, the temple, the open road, the foreign land—to get closer to the truth, which might be another way of saying *to get closer to danger*. Our term *truth*, we should note, derives from the Old English word *triewð*, meaning "faith, faithfulness, pledge, loyalty."[6] Triewð is perhaps closer to our word *trust*[7] (and both *truth* and *trust* are derived from the same proto-Indo-European word, *deru*). The searching man wants truth, not facts per se. Whether he goes it alone or as part of a group, a brotherhood, or a tribe, he wants to live as a hero at the heart of an unfolding myth that embodies and reveals to him something timeless, something beyond him that makes sense of everything.

In the "Hávamál," the god Odin says that he hung himself on a tree for nine nights, offering himself to Odin ("myself to myself").[8] It is through this act of self-sacrifice that he discovers the runes, or Mysteries, in what we must assume was some kind of vision or opening up of the consciousness. Yet in Odin's self-sacrifice ("myself to myself"), there is a strong suggestion that the god sacrifices some lower aspect of his being to his highest aspect. In human terms, this is the sacrifice of the lower self, the ego, to the Higher Self, the Atman, or the soul—to that divine spark of consciousness within that unites him with, or that is at the same time part of, God or Brahman. But in the world of the everyday, sacrificing "myself to myself" might also imply giving up our time or energy to become the kind of person we are aiming to become. The individual will have an image of that future self. Perhaps he sees himself as physically stronger, as a smartly dressed entrepreneur, or as a professor helping his students not merely to learn a particular subject but also to learn to think. But regardless, he sacrifices his time and effort to that image.

When an individual pushes himself beyond himself, becoming stronger, more skillful, or more learned, it is not merely because he wants to embody his highest potential in a particular area. It also is because he desires, if unconsciously, to discover that emptiness, that stillness and inner peace that is the Lord—the vastness of being—within him. The triewð, the pledge, he makes with the Lord and the faith, faithfulness, and loyalty he shows Him are sealed in the experience of inner peace in his life of struggle.

In the "Hávamál," Odin says that as he hung on the tree for nine nights, no one gave him food or drink. He looked "below," and "screaming," he took the runes. Then he "fell back" or collapsed. There is a palpable sense here of suffering and of pushing through the suffering. But Odin's looking "below" probably does not mean that he stared at the ground. Rather, it almost certainly implies that he stared into the depths, the abyss, or the void—that place where the consciousness of the individual meets the Consciousness of the cosmos or the Creator. And it is in this condition, of peering into the depths, that he discovers or understands the Mysteries.

There is another myth of struggle and revelation that is of relevance here. In the Bhagavad Gita, Krishna and his disciple Arjuna are waiting on the battlefield, ready to engage in battle against an invading army that includes a number of Arjuna's relatives. Arjuna protests that he does not want to fight, but Krishna insists that he must. Then Krishna—the Godhead—reveals his celestial form to his disciple and appears before him with millions of heads, arms, and legs, with the sun and moon as his eyes, and with all of creation, life and death, going on within his body. (Note that Krishna reveals his celestial form on the battlefield and not in a peaceful temple, grove, or mountain retreat.)

Let's just consider this statement that the sun and moon are the eyes of Krishna for a moment. And let's consider it from the perspective of premodern man, who lacked the technology to see the stars through a telescope or in photos brought back from a satellite. In modern spiritual circles, the sun and moon are often thought of as symbols of illumination and reflective consciousness (the sun illuminates and, of course, the moon reflects the light of the sun) or as representing the divine masculine and the divine feminine. But more important here, the sun and moon do not appear in the sky together. They are a vast distance apart—too far to be visible to us at the same time, except on rare occasions. If the eyes of Krishna are so far apart that we cannot see them both, then his body is beyond what we can imagine. It itself is vastness—the living, empty expanse of the sky, the universe, or the multiverse. And yet Krishna is also within us. Within us, there is a vast expanse (the "microcosm") that reflects that universe outside of us (the "macrocosm").

When Krishna tells Arjuna that he must fight in the battle whether he likes it or not, he tells him something of great importance that is easily overlooked or misunderstood. Krishna tells Arjuna that when he is on the battlefield, striking the enemy down, it will be Krishna who really strikes the enemy. Arjuna is just the instrument. The Godhead is what moves him and moves through him. The Godhead is at the very center of Arjuna and at the center of all things.

"Life is warfare," said Emperor Aurelius.[9] But who is waging the war of your life? Your ego? Or that inner calmness, the depth, the void, the daemon, the little god within, the meeting point of you and God? The rational is not enough. Indeed, it is easily turned into rationalizing and justifying our fears. Instead, we need vision, hope, conviction, will, or faith. To push through dark times, we often need what is not rational.

But faith, too, can be misused. Most people use "coping mechanisms" to "manage their anxiety," says Justin Menkes in *Better under Pressure*. "They ignore critical facts," he says, "while relying on a belief that things will work out."[10] We need to face the facts, no matter how difficult they may be, while having faith that we can come through. The problem, of course, is that sometimes the facts might suggest that we can't.

Just as we have considered positive thinking, visualization, and self-talk as part of the process of accomplishing what we want and need to accomplish, so prayer has its role, especially in times of great stress or fear. There is a practice in the Russian martial art of *systema* (the system) in which a practitioner will hold his breath for an extended amount of time. To overcome discomfort and panic (even if self-inflicted) and, crucially, to push beyond his normal capacity, the practitioner repeats the prayer "Lord have mercy" while holding his breath.[11] Prayer helps the individual to push through challenges because it affirms that not only is he *not* alone, he has God with him.

In *The Naked Ape*, Desmond Morris makes a claim about God that might be historically questionable but that has much merit psychologically. To give the background to the claim, Morris suggests that as our ancient ancestors left other forest-dwelling primates behind and struck out into new terrain, turning from vegetarian to hunter, it became important that the group cooperated closely. Our vegetarian ancestors were able to simply pick fruit from a nearby tree, but as hunters, they had to work together to capture or kill an animal that was often far stronger, bigger, faster, and more deadly than any human. Acceptance of the leader and his position was no longer enough. In these new circumstances, the leader needed the active support of the tribe and, more especially, of the hunting party.

Unlike the tyrannical primate leader of his ancestors and ours, who could pretty much do whatever he wanted with no repercussions, the tribal leader had to be seen as a cooperative member of the group. Even if he led the hunting party or made decisions for the tribe, he could not act as a tyrant. Yet, says Morris, psychologically, "there remained a need for an all-powerful figure who could keep the group under control, and the vacancy was filled by the invention of a god. The influence of the invented god-figure could then operate as a force additional to the now more restricted influence of the group leader."[12]

It is impossible for us to know what the first gods or goddess were like or when exactly man started believing in supernatural beings, but it is certainly true that—at least if we look at the oldest myths that we know of today, which rarely date back more than a few thousand years— ancient peoples often believed in a dominating god (Osiris, Zeus, Odin, etc.) among other gods and goddesses. But their powers were generally limited in comparison with the all-powerful gods of Zoroastrianism, Judaism, Christianity, or Islam, later on.

Yet Morris is correct that the god was seen as a kind of supernatural leader and that it acted—at least psychologically for the believer—as an additional force over and above the tribe and its leader (though a tribal king would often claim to be descended from a god or chosen by a god, while the pharaoh was regarded as a living god). On the battlefield, Krishna—the Godhead—is also very much the war leader and pushes Arjuna to fight even though he does not want to.

There are many other notable examples of a god inspiring men in times of battle. The ancient Norse warriors would throw a spear over the heads of the enemy when they met for battle, symbolically or ritually sacrificing the foe to Odin. And Constantine the Great (272–337 CE) had a vision of a cross of light (a sign of Christ) and the Greek phrase "ἐν τούτῳ νίκα" ("in this sign you shall conquer")* before going on to defeat his rival Maxentius at Milvian Bridge in Rome in 312 CE. A little over a millennia later, in 1412, Joan d'Arc, an illiterate peasant girl born in the village of Domrémy, France, would begin hearing voices at the age of thirteen. Believing them to be messages from God and soon believing that her mission from God was to lead the beleaguered French forces to victory against the invading English, Joan traveled to the court of the Dauphin, Charles, and convinced him to let her lead an army at Orléans. Incredibly, Joan was able to turn the war around and, despite a spate of French losses, led the French troops from one victory to another.

In behavioral psychology, there is a method of self-transformation called modeling. The patient finds someone that he wants to be more like and emulates that person. Perhaps it is an entrepreneur who wakes up early in the morning to work out or plan his day. Or perhaps he reads at least one book a week. Or perhaps he is good at listening to different opinions and thinking about the whole picture before com-

---

*Often translated into Latin as *In hoc signo vinces*.

ing to a decision. The patient takes up these habits. In some cases, he might imagine how it feels to be the individual he is modeling—how he stands, walks, or speaks.

If we are modeling someone or if we have a mentor, guru, or someone else we respect in our life, we can, of course, ask that person for advice. But often, once we've formulated the question we want to ask, we already know what the other person will say, and we refrain from asking; hence, the other's presence and our contemplation of the strengths and good qualities of that individual have the effect of drawing out the higher consciousness in us as we emulate that person. In prayer, God becomes the higher consciousness. We cannot model ourselves on God, of course, but in our minds, He nonetheless retains an element of the "all-powerful" leader that Morris speaks of. Hence, if we ask for God's help, it will not be for something trivial, or foolish, or that we think will be damaging to us. If we think about what God wants us to do in regard to a problem we are facing, the answer will be to act bravely, honestly, with confidence, with calmness, and for the best outcome. In other words, it will be to act as if God—the "all-powerful" leader—is with us. Instead of giving in to our cravings and weaknesses, we find that peace, calmness, and emptiness at the center of our being.

Try the following. Sit comfortably, close your eyes, and relax. Imagine the vastness of God. Thank Him for all the good things in your life, no matter how small—the habit you broke, the fact that you took some small action to improve yourself or your life despite all the obstacles, the beautiful weather, or the health of family members. Thank Him for giving you all this.

(If you're an atheist, imagine the vastness of the universe. See yourself as a mere speck of dust in comparison with it. Think of the mechanisms or laws of the universe that keep everything in harmony. Imagine this as a great "Mind" or as an "Intelligence." Try to feel that your consciousness is in communion with this great consciousness. Give thanks that the laws of creation and the consciousness behind them have worked to supply you with the good things in your life.)

Next, ask God (or if you're an atheist, ask the universe)* for help with the challenges you are facing. Mentally, state clearly what you want and need to happen. Ask for help in taking action, including in regard to the specific actions you need to take. Break large tasks down into smaller tasks if you can, and be clear in your mind about what those lesser tasks are as well. Then, once you've done that, give thanks for the aid you hope to receive.

Do this every day *while actively taking steps to get control of your situation and to overcome it.* Your prayer should *not* be a substitute for doing the work. It should bolster you emotionally so that you can face your fear with greater confidence and calm. Taking consistent action is the key. Especially when you are afraid, break things down into small steps so you can move toward your fear with minimum risk, gaining confidence and becoming more able, physically and mentally, to cope with the pressure and better able to deal with any problem that might arise. With each successful small step, you will gain the necessary confidence to go on.

Having spoken about prayer, before we leave the subject of fear, let's briefly look at meditation. Earlier, we described life as thinly disguised chaos. And we've also spoken of the calmness, the void, the Higher Self at the center of our being and, as such, at the center of the chaos around us. In the Japanese martial arts, there is the concept of "No Mind" or

---

*I am not suggesting that God and the universe are equivalent.

"No-Mind-No-Thought." Zen master Takuan Soho says that this Mind appears when we are "facing a time of need."[13]

In Japanese ink painting, there is a practice of painting a circle with a single movement while exhaling. If the painter is calm, focused, and absorbed in the act of painting—or we might say, if he has a state of No Mind—he might produce an image that is not only circular but that also appears smooth and flowing, reflecting the movement of the brush, which is, in turn, guided by the hand, the breath, and the mind. But if doubt enters his consciousness or if he loses concentration, even for a split second—if he is in a state of what Soho calls the "Confused Mind"—the circle will be uneven or will appear lumpy and awkward, more like the outline of a boulder than a circle.

But why would we be able to enter a state of No Mind when we are "facing a time of need"? Fear can either overwhelm us or focus us. If the threat or challenge is immediate, such as having to spar with a far more advanced martial artist or having to get up on stage to give a talk, we might forget most of the martial arts techniques we have learned or we might forget our speech. But fear also means that distracting, mundane thoughts are pushed aside. We are totally in the moment, totally focused on what we are confronting. And if we can control our fear and can focus on what we need to do rather than on how afraid we are, it can aid our performance.

If the threat is slower burning, such as facing a long-term financial struggle, we can become overwhelmed by stress and anxiety. We might feel that we are unable to take meaningful action. And more than a few people will seek to distract themselves with drink, drugs, or some other escape. But here, too, we must turn our focus toward what we can do and take action. Perhaps we cannot work on the major problem facing us for every hour of the day. But we can create a strong routine to get control of our days, working out regularly, meditating, reading, and improving ourselves as much as we can and, crucially, seeing that improvement and recognizing that we do still have control over who we are.

Focus takes practice. In awareness meditation, the meditator will focus his attention on the breath. As he breathes in, he will say to himself "breathing in" or "inhaling." As he exhales, he will say to himself "exhaling" or "breathing out." If he starts to feel discomfort in some part of his body, he will say to himself "sensation." And if he hears a noise, he will say "noise." But he will not get caught up in the stimuli. He does not, for example, think to himself that the discomfort is annoying or that meditation is uncomfortable or that he could be doing something more pleasurable and then think about what he could be doing or whom he could be doing it with. He just returns to focusing on the breath.

Stimuli arise in the consciousness in the form of thoughts and fantasies and outside of us in our daily lives. And there is a strong element of chaos, randomness, or entropy in both. Chögyam Trungpa has said that instead of using meditation to avoid problems, we should use it to discover our own attempts at self-deception,[14] looking at ourselves honestly.[15] Similarly, in regard to external stimuli, Menkes says that to be aware of circumstances that he is in, the leader has to have an "utter absence of shame" about his own miscalculations and failures when navigating all of these "stimuli."[16] There is chaos. Yet this chaos is the foundation for every possibility, bad or good, and for every opportunity, lost or taken. It is what the Greeks and Romans called Fate. And only by accepting that it is a part of life and being able to go out into the unknown, facing challenges, finding possibility in chaos, finding the faith to overcome fear, and turning fate into destiny will we ever discover who we truly are.

8

VENTURING INTO THE
GREAT UNKNOWN

SOCIETY TRIES TO PROTECT ITSELF from nature and from chaos. Yet they intervene. Gawain is challenged by the Green Knight. And to keep his word to the stranger and to find the Green Chapel, he is forced to journey for a whole year through strange lands, dense forests, and unfamiliar terrain. Before he departs Arthur's kingdom, Gawain is given a shield on which is painted a pentangle, or five-pointed star, described as a sign invented by King Solomon. The significance of the five-pointed star has multiple layers. It represents, we are told, the five senses, in regard to which Gawain was found to be faultless.[1] It signifies fellowship, generosity, courtesy, compassion, and purity,[2] which Gawain is said to embody. And it represents the strength of Gawain's four fingers and thumb[3]—indicative of physical health and strength and the ability to grip a sword or horse's reins. But the pentangle also represents the knight's faith in the five wounds of Christ on the cross and the five joys that the "Queen of Heaven" felt for her child. Moreover, we are told that whenever Gawain is in battle, he is fortified by thinking of those joys and, hence, of Jesus and Mary. The earthly and the holy are related.

Symbolically, the five senses and the five digits of the hand are related to the five wounds of Christ and the five joys of Mary. The sacred is, in some sense, reflected in the mundane, and vice versa.

The five virtues (fellowship, generosity, courtesy, compassion, and purity) run through the legend. We have already explored fellowship, or the need to be part of a group. Like the other knights and like all other human beings, Gawain is a social creature. He celebrates the season with others and feels joy. We should not dismiss this too lightly. It is all too easy to make oneself into a misfit, to see oneself as someone whom others cannot understand, and to separate from society.

Yet the initiatic path leads into the unknown and therefore into a total freedom. The Green Knight has told Gawain to look for the Green Chapel and to ask others along his journey where it might be found. The knight has no knowledge of where it might be and no map. To find the Green Chapel—and to find himself—he must first lose himself.

Before he leaves, the courtiers are full of sorrow and worry about the fate that appears to await Gawain. Perhaps he will not survive. Gawain tells them, simply, that "a man's fate" must be tested.[4] He must leave the knights of the Round Table, the ladies, and Guinevere and go into a hostile and alien environment. Traveling through the wilds, he becomes, in effect, an outlaw, a man outside the laws of the community, town, or society. Other humans exist only here and there, and each one is an enemy—perhaps a robber lurking at a bridge or crossroads.

Nietzsche believed that good and evil were one in nature, but that they had been cleaved from it and separated by religious authorities who posited a Creator separate from His Creation and by the philosophers who, like the priests, presented moral values contrary to that of aristocratic strength and action.[5] The philosophers aimed to produce a good, happy, or wise man and the religions an obedient one. But traveling alone through unknown lands, through nature, where the laws of man cannot be applied, Gawain can be neither good nor evil. Contemplating his fate at the hands of the Green Knight, he will not be happy. And the journey itself, which as far as Gawain knows is a journey to his death, might not be wise. The knight has plunged himself into that primordial condition that existed before society, before good and evil. It is a place of absolute Being, where threats to his individual life are everywhere. Out in this freedom, he has total responsibility, not only for his safety but also to get to his destination.

Why must the knight go out into the wild? Why is this so necessary? G. K. Chesterton claimed that we need a life of "practical romance"—a life that combined mystery and practicality.[6] We, of course, have come to associate "romance" with personal love, expressed through candlelit dinners and holding hands while walking on the beach. Yet the romantic nature of men is different. As we will see later, it is archetypally fixed on death, nature, the void, order, and the heroic. It can be expressed in going out into the wilds, the unknown, into a vastness that might kill the undisciplined adventurer or in building the monumental. A man wants to confront vastness itself, to glimpse, in a sense, the face of God moving on the unknown.

In fact, the word *romance* originally referred to tales of chivalry and the adventures of knights and only much later began to refer to love. The male romantic spirit is embodied not only in such tales as *Sir Gawain and the Green Knight* but also in such works of art as Frederic Edwin Church's paintings of icebergs, with their primordial mountains of ice and emerald-green-lit caverns, as if an entrance to another world, and in Arnold Böcklin's painting *Isle of the Dead,* in which a ferryman approaches a mysterious island of rock and trees.

Initiation into manhood, or into the Mysteries of life, means moving into this space of unknowing and risk, of acceptance of our death and of our own responsibility for our life and actions. This requires moving into the wilds, into the dark forest, into our own shadow, into what we do not want to face. There is light at the end, but we cannot reach it strolling through a meadow of flowers.

Male initiatic societies exist in most cultures. These often restrict initiations to boys who have reached puberty and who are regarded by the tribe as reaching manhood or to men who have considerably passed puberty. In some cases, a boy will leave his mother's house at puberty and will then go to live with the father. As we have mentioned, in Sparta, boys were taken from their mothers at the age of seven and initiated into the agoge. We, too, must leave the nurturing environment of our home, especially of the mother—who wants to protect us, who does not want to look at our faults, and who will even be prepared to make excuses for us—and we must engage the world as it is, which might not accord with our sense of right and wrong, our belief in fairness, or our understanding of how we should behave.

It is natural to worry about those we love. But every time someone worries about us, they signal that we might not be able to cope with the situation after all. When the mother openly worries about the son, she signals not only her love for him but also, perhaps more strongly, a doubt that he can cope the way other men do. For the son, this can prove debilitating.

There is a story of a merchant in Japan. He had diligently learned the martial art of grappling, restraining, and empty-hand escape techniques. One night, a samurai who had fallen on hard times and was living as a down-and-out broke into the merchant's house to steal from him. When the merchant tried to resist, the intruder became angry and insulted him for being a merchant. Hearing the insult, the merchant felt overwhelmed and completely forgot about his training. Who, after all, was he to take on a samurai? Then his wife shouted that he was not a merchant but that he was a martial artist. When he heard this, he regained his composure and fought off the intruder.[7]

Notice that the wife did not scream with fear, either for her safety or her husband's. The fellowship we need to foster is like that: we need close friends and perhaps a group who will encourage us to be, and to do, our best, pushing us out of our comfort zone, helping us to overcome our weaknesses, encouraging us to take manageable risks, and reminding us of our strengths when we face a crisis.

In martial arts training, the techniques that are taught generally become progressively more difficult. A student might begin by learning a straight kick, then a roundhouse kick, then a 360-degree kick, then a jumping (or "flying") kick, then a jumping roundhouse kick. There is little risk of injury in practicing a straight kick. There is a little more risk of losing one's balance and falling with a roundhouse kick, and even more with a jumping roundhouse kick. But the increasing risk is offset by the growth in the student's skill and balance. Nevertheless, while a martial arts school will help the student to avoid getting injured, the instructor will normally treat the student as if he is capable of suffering an injury without becoming overwhelmed. And many schools will expect an injured student to continue to train if he can do so without making it worse.

But let's take another example of facing some risk. Most people are afraid of having to speak in public. The first time an individual delivers a talk in public, he can rehearse until he has more or less memorized what he wants to say. Later, he will be able to speak in public with little or no preparation but with greater confidence. Again, in learning, we have to contemplate what is relatively simple at first and move to more complex ideas later on, even if we don't know exactly where the journey will take us. Indeed, at a certain point, an individual who has mastered a certain field will break away from the accepted dogma or rules and will propose his own theory, found a new art movement, or develop a new style of martial arts. Such a journey requires us to build resilience, to be able to face new and more complex challenges, and to gain confidence. And it also requires us to be genuinely interested and engaged in what we are doing so that we can solve the puzzle that others have not noticed and can contribute something new.

Like Gawain, we must seek without a map, accepting that the world embodies what the alchemists referred to as "chaos"—a primordial churning of energy and events that offers us unlimited possibilities, good and bad, including for our own elevation and for our own destruction. But we must also accept that such a place, though chaotic and entropic, is ultimately meaningful. It is the realm of initiation and the place where we will come face-to-face with our true nature and, as such, with our Creator. We are afraid of this total freedom because we fear that we might not measure up to whatever comes at us out of the dark. We fear that we will fail. Or perhaps we fear that we will not only fail but that we also will accept failure and will not try again.

Freedom, as Eric Hoffer observed, is felt as both a blessing and a "burden." The burden the individual bears is that the "blame of failure" for his action or inaction is placed on his shoulders alone. He has to live with the consequences of what he does or what he refuses to do. In *Sir Gawain and the Green Knight,* the landscape through which Gawain travels is thoroughly different from the castle of the knights of the Round Table. There, in the banquet hall, he had sat next to Guinevere. Out in the country, he faces bandits and robbers at every turn or every bridge. He has only himself to rely on and only himself to blame. There can be no obfuscation, no finger-pointing, no blaming of parents or society.

There is a story of two Zen monks, Nyogen Senzaki and his teacher Soyen Shaku. The two men left Japan for America in 1905, partly to escape the growing Japanese nationalist movement. But once there, Senzaki liked America and came to hope that he would remain in the country. Sensing his desire, one day, in San Francisco, Shaku asked his disciple to go for a walk to Golden Gate Park. There, Shaku put down Senzaki's suitcase and spoke to him, telling him to see if he would defeat the city or whether the city would defeat him. Then the master walked off, never to see the disciple again.[8] Senzaki went on to become one of the most prominent Zen Buddhists in America.

We have to go into the unknown. This might be into the wilderness or into the city. As with Nyogen Senzaki, it might mean leaving one's home country. Or it might mean moving from one town or city to another. In other cases, it will mean listening to and considering opinions we do not like. In a few cases, it may mean formal initiation into a society or brotherhood that has its own rules, expectations, and set of standards.

But what, we should ask, are we likely to take with us when we travel into the unknown? Our status in society will be useless. Our moral posturing will win us no applause. The bad habits we have developed to get us through the day will no longer be possible. If we truly prepare ourselves for the unknown, we will pack light, taking only what we need to survive physically, mentally, and spiritually. We will shift our thinking from virtues to *virtus*. We will move away from the belief that society will protect us and toward the desert values or frontier values.

Besides traveling to a new city or a new land and testing ourselves in the alien environment, ritual initiation has also provided a way into the unknown. Such rituals have existed in probably all ancient and traditional cultures. During the initiation ritual of Craft Freemasonry, the initiate is not allowed to keep anything metal on him and, in fact, does not enter the lodge room with any possessions. Traditionally, this meant money and weapons, or more broadly speaking, it meant tools. In the movie *Easy Rider* (1969), two bikers named Wyatt and Billy travel across the United States from Los Angeles to New Orleans, encountering various alternative lifestyle communities as well as bigotry and violence because of their bohemian appearance and way of life. At the beginning of the movie, Wyatt does something of great symbolic value: he takes off his wristwatch and throws it away. Time no longer matters. Material luxuries no longer matter.

Whether they are aware of it or not, the trip Wyatt and Billy are about to undertake is initiatic. Like Gawain, they will have to live by their wits, skill, and character. But the initiatic action also means facing one's own death. Gawain travels to the Green Chapel with the full belief that he will be killed. The initiate to Freemasonry must contemplate his own mortality (and in some jurisdictions is required to sit in a Chamber of Reflection in which will be placed the symbol of a skull). And in *Easy Rider*, when the two twentieth-century outlaws visit a brothel, Wyatt has a premonition of his death—a second-long scene of his motorcycle on fire by the side of a road—when he looks at a painting of a scroll on which the essayist Joseph Addison is quoted: "Death only closes a man's reputation and determines it as good or bad." To step into the wilderness, the unknown, into a place without time is to enter into a world of the archetypal, a world not of entertainment, consuming, and passing the time but of death and sex and heightened consciousness.

Unsurprisingly, perhaps, many are unwilling to go into the

unknown, whether into the wild or into the city or into a martial arts temple or into a spiritual school. Instead, as Hoffer notes, the individual attempts to escape the awesome burden of freedom by immersing himself in a mass movement.[9] The "mass" quality is important. Unlike a group of ten, twenty, thirty, forty or so—a dojo, a lodge, a chapter, a spiritual circle, a social circle—a mass is anonymous. And the individual wants to lose himself in it; to be caught up in the crowd; to act as part of a wave, a surge of energy; to be a voice—and sometimes a fist—for the ideology he has adopted without question; and to be blameless for his actions, since they are not really his. Paradoxically, freedom means self-responsibility. It requires us to try again and again in all different areas of life; consequently, we must experience failure again and again throughout our life.

We spoke earlier of Gawain losing himself in the wilds to find himself. By this we mean that he—and the initiate—must cast off his self-image, which will have helped him in the limited circumstances of his life but that no longer serves him once he is out in the unknown. He must cast off this small "self" in order to realize and give shape to the power he has within. Perhaps an individual is insecure about his intelligence and goes out of his way to prove how academic he is. He sticks to the rules, writes and speaks in an academic manner. Then something happens inside. He steps into the unknown and delivers a talk with feeling and passion, mesmerizing or uplifting the audience. Or perhaps he thinks of himself as clumsy or as somehow not physical. Yet in the dojo, after months or years of practice, at the sudden command of his sensei, he sees his own fist flying through the air, breaking a wooden board in front of him. He saw it happen and is amazed at the ease at which he broke it. But it seems to him that it was not he who broke it, but rather that something moved through him.

Yet as we have said, there will be failures along the way. Some of these failures may be small and personal, others large and impersonal, but they impact us all the same. We must question ourselves, adjust, reinvent ourselves, and uncover our weaknesses, recognizing even that what served us well a decade ago may have become an obstacle to us now. To move forward through life is to recognize an inherent chaos, instability, and constant change.

Spirituality is discovered and tested in the ordinary world. When Chan Buddhism entered Japan from China (becoming known as Zen Buddhism), the language barrier forced the monks to think creatively about how to communicate complex ideas in a simple way. And they began teaching Zen through everyday activities: polishing a mirror, the tea ceremony, or the martial arts. Likewise, Freemasonry teaches about the nature of man and the Nature of God by making building and architectural tools into metaphors and symbols. In general, though, we have lost the ability of premodern man to see life as the unfolding of a great miracle or as a description of how we can seek enlightenment. Nor do we see the Mystery in ordinary things.

Whether we want deep self-knowledge or mystical experience, we must begin with the mundane, examining our being and uncovering our physical, mental, and emotional weaknesses. If we are physically weak, we need to work on gaining physical strength. And this is especially the case if we have come to see our self as intellectual, sophisticated, and above the sort of man who prizes physical strength. If we have difficulty either expressing or containing our emotions, we must work to rectify this, too. And if we have adopted a theory about life, then we must seek out the most intelligent representatives of the opposite view.

We are always told that we cannot go beyond certain bounds for knowledge, that reading a certain book or author or not agreeing with those of lesser knowledge makes us somehow suspect or outside the fold of the moral collective. Doubtlessly, this is not a new phenomenon. You must ignore the critics and the cynics and become a creator. This requires both depth and breadth of knowledge. Explore different fields and find the connections between them. Study the most intelligent and thoughtful exponents of beliefs you disagree with. Listen to them while being open to changing your mind, with the intention of wanting to learn why they think what they do.

Your aim is neither to agree or to disagree. It is to not be a cliché, fitting in here or there. It is to come to your own conclusions, to think differently from others because you understand more deeply and have contemplated what others have ignored. Quality of thinking is improved only when there is challenge. Hence, the fifteenth-century philosopher and kabbalist Pico della Mirandola claimed that the Chaldeans believed a future philosopher should be born when the planet Mars (associated with war) would "behold" Mercury (associated with communication), because without war, all philosophy would become "drowsy."[10]

Only when Mars and Mercury, ferocity and meekness, the gymnast and the musician, the warrior and the creative individual come together in us will we rise above the clichés of our own time, become larger than life or, rather, embody life. We want "muscles and nerves of steel" and a mind that is their equivalent so that we are able to wade into reality without drowning, experiencing life fully—our heart pumping, our mind alert, and our being energized.

Listen to your opponent, and, yes, you might disagree with 99 percent of what he says. So what? You must be capable of hearing things you do not like. Use the experience to improve your own arguments and, far more importantly, to more clearly understand why you think what you do. If you find that you agree with one percent or with one single idea, take it and see how it improves your thinking or your life or how it might lead you to a new area of exploration, one that is neither his nor yours. Take every encounter as an adventure.

Like the weight lifter who gains muscle through struggling to lift heavier and heavier weights, so you can only develop your mind by encountering and seriously considering different ideas. And make no mistake, no matter how intelligent or enlightened you may think you are, the world contains beliefs, ideas, ideologies, and practices of which you know nothing. If others refuse to hear arguments against their beliefs, that is all the better for you. You will exceed them.

9

THE MECHANICAL WORLD
AND THE
PRIMORDIAL WORLD

WE HAVE SAID GOODBYE to the safety and security of the childhood home and have gone out into the world and into the unknown. But what is the character of the world in which we now find ourselves? And what is our relationship to it? We must address these questions if we are going to transform and elevate ourselves and our lives.

It is with the discovery of modern mathematics and the invention of the telescope that the modern era begins, says Jean Baudrillard. With these, man both observed the planets in the distant sky and alienated himself from nature—from the nature that he depended on and had always been a part of.[1] He observed life, the world—the cosmos itself, even—from a new vantage point that placed him outside of its activity. In a sense, he became the equivalent of God. For if God had created the material cosmos, man—the scientist—now observed it at a distance.

Observing even the birth and death of stars and galaxies millions of light years away, man had become the observer par excellence. He had adopted a new identity. He was no longer a creature created by the Divine and made in the image of the Divine, but rather, in his ultimate expression, he was the critic. He was the animal that could peer into, that could theorize, and that could know, not by doing, not by being a part of something, not by creating something, but by thinking about and by being separate from something. He became the *cosmic* critic.

In premodern times, the world was, of course, conceived of as having been made by God or by the gods. And while the world was full of the supernatural, the abode of God or the gods was out there, in the sky, among clouds and stars. Hence, Michelangelo's *Last Judgment* fresco in the Sistine Chapel. In it, a multitude of figures are depicted around the central figures of Christ and Mary. Actors in a cosmic drama, the figures sprawl across clouds that resemble lumps of dough.

Clouds were not the subject of serious study for artists. Yet later, in the work of British artist John Constable (1776–1837), the sky changes. His rival, William Turner, painted clouds as elemental, storm-like mirages set on fire by the sun. They were dramatic and primordial, mythic and visionary, but they were still unreal. Constable was the first artist to paint the sky as it was, making studies of clouds and even socializing with meteorologists and learning about the burgeoning science of meteorology from them.

It is possible to see the wrath or power of God in Turner's clouds, but Constable has expelled the sacred. His clouds are exquisitely painted, but they are clouds like any other. To put it bluntly, Constable takes us up into a sky where there is no God and no Mystery, only air and moisture. He turns the sky into a no-man's-land. But only temporarily. For with the invention of the airplane, man displaces the angels and makes the sky *his* abode. Or to put it another way, he makes the sky the realm of fact and not the imagination. With modernity, it has become merely a vast sheet dissected by invisible flight paths and measured according to humidity, wind speed, and so on. To imagine and dream again, we now look beyond the sky, to Mars.

There is another painting of relevance here: *Nose-Diving on the City* by futurist painter Tullio Crali. This strange work depicts the inside of a fighter plane's cockpit as the plane is descending on a city in which every building is a variation on the cube. The sky and the earth are dominated by modern technology, though—if perhaps futilely—the architect and the pilot have both attempted to embody the heroic, visionary spirit through the use of technology. But Crali's painting is important for another reason. We see the back of the head of the pilot. It is not a portrait. He is anonymous. Or really, he is a proxy for whoever is looking at the painting. Even if we can no longer imagine the gods in the night sky, we can imagine ourselves in the cockpit, flying the plane. We can imagine ourselves as pioneers building a new world.

In the modern era, then, man goes both outward into the sky and space and inward through the psychology of Carl Jung and Sigmund Freud, into his own psyche. And he desacralizes both. Crali's is only one painting that shows a figure from behind. Of course, there had been depictions of the back of the human form prior to the modern era, but they were typically female nudes, and the viewer was supposed to appreciate the beauty of the figure—or to be aroused by it—rather than to identify with it. Modern paintings of the backs of figures are psychological. And from Caspar David Friedrich's *Wanderer above the Sea of Fog* and René Magritte's *Not to Be Reproduced* and *Decalcomania* to Andrew Wyeth's *Christina's World*, they are often among the artist's best-known works. Notably, Swiss symbolist painter Arnold Böcklin painted no less than five versions of his celebrated *Isle of The Dead*, which depicts a ferryman, seen from behind, rowing toward a mysterious and shadowy isle. And tellingly, a reproduction hung in Freud's study.[2]

Man has gone from finding meaning out there in the sky, where the angels resided, and in the forest, where a green knight might be traveling or where nature spirits might dwell, to finding meaning inside of the individual himself. For Baudrillard, as soon as modern man, with his highly developed intellectual faculty, gave meaning to the world, he began, at the same time, to dissolve it, though this is only true in the modern, material understanding of the meaning of weight and measure. He analyzed,* broke, or cut each thing into segments, dissected the world, and named each part. And through this act of naming, he robbed each thing of its own vitality.[3] Truth became debatable. Hence, in Magritte's *Treachery of Images,* we see a gentleman's pipe above the words, *"Ceci n'est pas une pipe"* (This is not a pipe). A pipe is a real thing, but Magritte reminds us that the image of the pipe is not real, but only an image—only paint on canvas. Only an illusion.

But if Magritte's pipe is not a real pipe, his words are nonetheless real words. (Or at least, the words in the painting [*"Ceci n'est pas une pipe"*] are more authoritative than the image and tell us about the image.) We have stepped into a world where words and conceptions are more real than the real things—and people—around us.

"Mythology is inevitable, it is natural, it is an inherent necessity of language," says Ernst Cassirer.[4] But mythology has a symbiotic relationship with existence. It shapes human culture, but it is also shaped by human culture and by the human conception of nature. It represents them and tells us how we should act in regard to other human beings,

---

*Baudrillard reminds us that *analyze* means "dissolve."

nature, and our own Will. Not only myths but also art and words are used to represent reality. But as Cassirer points out, revealing as much about our own beliefs about reality as we do about reality itself, we inevitably "obscure" what we seek to "reveal." For "modern skeptical critics of language," then, Cassirer says, "Not only myth, art, and language, but even theoretical knowledge becomes a phantasmagoria."[5] For the modern individual, life is not presented *through* concepts but *becomes* a concept or a mixture of concepts. What matters is not *what is* but how we can frame it. From art to religion and from ethics to human biology, life itself becomes a "social construct."

The pipe is not a pipe. Dissecting everything and breaking each thing into its constituent parts, modern man's action is the antithesis of the Biblical narrative in which God creates all of the animals and all of the birds and then brings them to Adam to see what he will name them (Genesis 2:19–20). Adam names them whole. He names the lamb, not the leg of lamb, and not the brain, bones, or testicles of the lamb. And he names the whole of the animal kingdom. His aim is not to see the mechanics—the guts, the blood, how this organ is related to that—but to know the whole of the life that the Creator has created. Noah, too, brings not meat or parts but living animals onto the ark. It is not a science experiment. It is life.

The animal has a character. In a sense, it is an archetype: the stag is proud, the boar fierce, the fox cunning, and so on. Historically, a king might identify with a lion. Odin is associated with the raven and Christ with the lamb. The Hindu goddess Durga is usually depicted riding on the back of a lion or tiger, and the head of the Egyptian god Horus is that of a falcon. From the Norse úlfhéðnar to the elite Russian Spetsnaz, warriors and military groups have often associated themselves with wolves. To be among the animals, then, is to know what qualities the Creator established in physical form and what, too, might lie latent in man's own character.

Even in antiquity, of course, animals were killed, cut up, and eaten for food. Yet the people also lived with the animals that they ate. Hence, rituals were performed to make sure the animal was reborn and to ensure the blessings of the gods on their barbaric action. And today in the traditional butcher's shop (with its roots in premodernity), the whole carcass is strung up in the window, whereas the meat that is displayed in the modern supermarket—cut into small pieces, the blood cleaned away—is abstract and, in many cases, appears like small, round fruit. There are no full carcasses to remind the consumer what he is consuming.

Yet there is also this quality of observing, which we have mentioned. In academia, in the majority of cases, scholars believe that they must not practice or be a part of what they study because they must remain "objective." Popular entertainment is almost everywhere—the television, the movies, the internet, the giant electronic billboards in the center of cities. We do not necessarily want or need to watch remarkable people. Indeed, we will return again and again to television dramas that depict entirely ordinary lives, and we will follow the most ordinary of vloggers and look at, and like, photos of our friends' meals online.

Everything is becoming virtual. Spectator sports, from baseball to mixed martial arts, have become multibillion-dollar industries. Why? From the comfort of his home, the spectator is able to watch, cheer, scream, and consume junk food and beer while he watches. His heart races as the game or fight plays out before him. He may even comment about it with passion and conviction. He is certain that he knows what he would do if he were in the situation of this or that player or fighter. But in general, watching the game or fight is the closest he will come to experiencing it. He does not even understand the irony of scarfing down unhealthy food and drink as he watching his sporting hero, whose diet and training regimen is likely to be extremely strict. Sex too is increasingly virtual, and increasingly political, even as people—especially younger people—are having less actual sex.

In our observer culture, everything is moving around us: sport, sex, relationships. We watch a drama and become engaged in the lives of the characters, though we know that we are not a part of the drama. The relationships, the sexual scandals, the personal conflicts, the lies and confessions, and so on that keep us going back for more are not real. The unfolding events are merely images on a screen. The same occurs with politics. We eagerly consume lies and half-truths, passionately agree with the opinions du jour, and denounce whoever must be denounced. In our increasingly passionless lives, we are thus filled with passion and righteousness, though we keep quiet when our favorite politician breaks his word, changes his mind, or behaves exactly like the opposition. We are anti-war until our political party starts a war. Then we pretend not to notice the death toll.

When we are driving in a car, we can see—and our inner ears can detect—that we are moving, though we are not running or jumping, but sitting. Our body is not moving us. Something else is moving us, and we are a spectator to it, watching things pass us by. For some people, of course, this causes motion sickness. And perhaps many in our society are suffering from a kind of cultural motion sickness—a sense of being on a merry-go-round and having no control over the ride (hence, the nearly forty million Americans suffering from anxiety disorders).[6]

Perhaps this is why we go to the concert to see musicians play live when we can play their music any time we like or go to the Louvre to see the *Mona Lisa* though we have seen the painting reproduced a thousand times before or why we want to get our favorite celebrity's signature. We want to feel that we are engaged in the real world, with real people, and that it is not a stream of moving images on a screen giving us a false sense of living—perhaps along with a sense of falling.

We have spoken about the modern inclination to dissect, to take apart, and to examine the parts. There is a curious diagram—a "picture" of the ordinary man—in Ouspensky's *Psychology of Man's Possible Evolution*. It is a circle dissected into several rows and columns of squares, and inside each square is a letter *I,* representative of the different selves held together in the "individual." If we want to look to popular culture to find a reflection of this idea, we will find it in Andy Warhol's silk-screen prints of Marlon Brando, Jackie Kennedy, and Marilyn Monroe. Unlike earlier portraits, these show the same image multiple times—four, six, or even sixteen of them—in a single work. Somehow, these different selves are held together, but we nonetheless feel the fragmentation. It has become part of our lives. In a single day, we move from the comfort of home, through the grime of the city subway train or stuck in a car on the highway, to the stark office of glass and blank white walls, and perhaps to a cafe or restaurant as well.

According to Gurdjieff, man consumes three different types of food: the food we eat (which feeds our bodies), air (which we take into our lungs and which feeds our emotions), and "impressions" (which enter us through the senses and which are needed by our intellect).[7] It should be obvious that your diet should be made up of natural, healthy food (preferably food that you have cooked yourself). And we all want to breathe clean air. But let's think about Gurdjieff's third type of food: impressions or aesthetics, which we consume primarily in the form of sight or sound.

We tend to think that the spiritual person isn't concerned with appearances. Yet the spiritual teacher Frithjof Schuon claimed that one of the "dimensions" of his teachings was "beauty: beauty of forms, of surroundings, of dress, of comportment."[8] In the Greek language, κᾰλός (*kalós*) means "beautiful," "good," and even "noble." Drawing on Wolfgang von Goethe, the Catholic theologian Josef Pieper has said that beauty is a "promise" rather than a "fulfilment."[9] When we see something of beauty—a beautiful woman, the beauty of nature, or a beautiful object—we are drawn to it. It mesmerizes us, seemingly promising to change our life or our inner being in some way, if only we could possess it. Yet, Pieper suggests, it cannot fulfill us in "our bodily existence." We forget our encounters with the sacred, but beauty makes us remember them.[10] And it makes us remember them by making us feel whole.

We must, then, be cautious about what impressions we consume since so much of what we consume visually or audibly makes us feel fragmented. Over a thousand years ago, the Persian physician, alchemist, and philosopher Abu Bakr Muḥammad ibn Zakariya' al-Razi (865–925 CE) warned against listening to sad, languid music or reading poetry or literature about love and sex.[11] Over a millennia later, we should also be cautious about hard-core pornography, as well any form of entertainment (including gossip and "news") that is depressing, makes us angry, stresses the negative, or makes us believe that we are victims of society, incapable of taking control of our own lives.

But what about the modern environment itself? According to Islamic tradition, the final hour of the world will have arrived when the buildings of Mecca reach as high as the mountains (thus towering over the Kaaba, sacred to Muslims).[12] As depicted in the biblical story of the Tower of Babel (which itself is depicted in the Tower card of the tarot, a signifier of ruin), the building that reaches to the sky signifies a loss of humility, competition with God, and thus confusion. But there is also an aesthetic element, which cannot be ignored.

Walk through any city in the West and the tower blocks and skyscrapers dwarf the church spires, which are, in many such cities, little more than relics from another era. Part of the spiritual confusion of the West comes from our immersion in the aesthetics of modernity and the loss of traditional aesthetics, in which the natural world remains present in the construction of buildings (stone and wood for walls, straw and reed for thatched roofs), in everyday tools (clay for bowls, iron for cooking pots), clothing (wool, cotton, linen), and food.

It is possible to be a brahmin in a village by the Ganges, a Shia Muslim in Najaf, and a Zen Buddhist in Kyoto. And though devotion might decline or grow over the generations, it is possible, too, even for the Hindu devotee who lives in the West or some other part of the world to remain a Hindu while the village remains the embodiment of Hindu aesthetics, for the Shiite who lives elsewhere to remain a Shiite while Najaf still embodies the aesthetics of Shiism, and for the Zen Buddhist to remain Zen Buddhist while Kyoto still embodies the aesthetics of Zen. And it is possible precisely because he can imagine the place where the aesthetics of the religion—its temples, art, rituals, and food—are embodied and because he has the assurance that it is not just his imagination: the place truly exists, and thus, the religion is still alive. When he performs a ritual or cooks a meal, he is an extension, a satellite, of that sacred place and not, as so many are in modernity, an atomized individual.

In Europe, early Christian churches were often built over pre-Christian sacred sites. And now the churches themselves are replaced by modern buildings or turned into spaces for secular purposes. But what is the faith of the high-rise, the shopping mall, and the superhighway?* The problem we face in the West is that there is no equivalent of Kyoto in most of its countries. The aesthetics we associate with Christianity (the cathedral, the village, the brown-robed friar, the knight, etc.) and with the pre-Christian peoples of Europe (nature, the sacred well, the sacred grove, etc.) have long been in retreat. Catholicism is still alive in Europe as something little more than an identity, partly because Rome and Lourdes remain ancient in appearance and because the religion has always cultivated aesthetics and—in contrast to Protestantism, which was against "idols"—has always been concerned with beauty.[13] For this reason, Catholicism is alive in South America, which adopted its saints and created an aesthetic of altars, statues, flowers, music, and parades.

In the West, with the loss of aesthetic localities (natural and ancient), there was a decline in religion. And with the decline in religion has come the loss of meaning, the loss of mystery, and the idea that truth is relative. To some degree, too, there has also been a loss of imagination. Sometimes consciously and sometimes unconsciously, the Western world has attempted to recover some or all of this, partly through religious reform, the creation of Evangelical Christianity, the revival or "reconstruction" of European pagan religion, the adoption of non-Western religion, new ageism and the hippie movement, comparative religious studies, and psychology (especially Jungian).

But for all that it has contributed—and despite Carl Jung's artistic practice—psychology keeps us too much in the realm of the intellect.

---

*This is not the only style possible in modernity, of course. Besides the growth of interest in more natural, traditionally made products and the emergence of environmentally friendly architecture, we can look to, among others, sculptors Richard Long and Andy Goldsworthy; the early work of fashion designer Issey Miyake; and the work of Isamu Noguchi, a designer of furniture, lighting, gardens, and architecture, for examples of an entirely different aesthetic.

Spirituality also inhabits the realm of the imaginary and the aesthetic, and while psychology is individual, an aesthetic experience is collective and communal. Traditionally suspicious of intellectuals and more interested in feelings, neopaganism has grasped this and, like the German Wandervogel movement of a little more than a century ago, has returned to nature partly as a protest against the banality of the modern built environment and partly as an aesthetic experience. The neopagan goes out into the forest to perform a ritual to a god or goddess that is supposed to inhabit the natural environment, or he brings the forest back into his home, displaying crystals, flowers, a small tree branch, a bowl of water, or herbs on an altar.

Yet as in the cold, concrete, modernist church, something is missing in the forest. In aesthetics, we experience what others have made and what others before us have experienced: a building, a garden, a painting, a candle, a song, a poem, or a meal. Perhaps the most aesthetic of experiences, though, is the religious, spiritual, or initiatic ritual. Through these, the individual is immersed in a world that is otherworldly, where the sounds are those of chanting, the recitation of religious texts, or singing; where the sights are those of the altar, an icon, symbols, and candles; where the scent is one of incense; and where each thing seen, heard, or experienced alludes to both a tradition that extends from past to present (and perhaps to the future as well) and to an ultimate reality beyond this world.

We have noted that Gurdjieff regarded impressions as a type of food, and we should note in this regard that while agriculture emerged around twelve thousand years ago, slowly eradicating the hunter-gatherer way of life, the earliest-surviving cave art (found in Europe and Indonesia) dates from around forty thousand years ago and the earliest-known musical instruments were created around forty-two to forty-three thousand years ago.*[14] The oldest-known jewelry was made around seventy-five thousand years ago near the Southern Cape shoreline in Africa.[15] In other words, humanity began cultivating aesthetics over sixty thousand years before it began to cultivate fruits, vegetables, or other crops. It seems that we need the aesthetic to feel fully alive. Indeed, just as we might feel physically ill after eating bad food, so we might feel stressed in an environment full of noise, grime, and ugly architecture (hence, the use of loud music and sight deprivation in "enhanced interrogation," also known as torture), and so too, we feel enlivened or at peace when we are somewhere beautiful. The harmonious makes us feel harmonious, and disharmony makes us feel disharmonious.

Despite modernity, we long for the natural and the primordial. We are mesmerized by images of the forest, the desert, the ocean, the stars, or the rugged landscape of Mars. And we want to find nature even in our own time. There are a few days over the summer when the setting sun is aligned with the streets of Manhattan. In an event that is known as Manhattanhenge, the sunlight bursts over the Hudson River and through the streets, between the high-rise buildings, in a glow of orange-gold. Crowds of city dwellers gather to watch the event, which is beautiful and reminiscent of something ancient and primordial (hence, the event's name alludes to the British prehistoric monument Stonehenge).

The modern world makes an encounter with natural beauty relatively rare. Usually, in the city, the sunrise and the sunset pass us by, hidden behind clusters of towering buildings. We do not see nature. A person might dress beautifully but act in a way that is ugly, getting drunk, trying to get attention, and so on. Beauty requires a certain detachment, a

---

*Two flutes found in what is now southern Germany, one made from bird bone and the other from mammoth bone.

certain calmness and composure. This does not mean that there can be no energy. A dancer might appear even more beautiful—and even more seductive—when dancing than when not. The dancer surrenders herself to the pattern of the movements yet remains composed.

We must acknowledge here something that we might call "male beauty." Traditionally, the term used to describe an attractive man is *handsome.* However, as it has been said, "Handsome is founded upon the notion of proportion, symmetry, as the result of cultivation or work; a handsome figure is strictly one that has been developed by attention to physical laws into the right proportions. It is less spiritual than beautiful."[16]

We are probably aware of what male ugliness is: inappropriate aggression (e.g., against women), violence against those who are weaker, drunkenness, scheming, cowardliness, a lack of self-awareness, and a lack of self-control and self-discipline. In regard to the physical, it is the untrained body (i.e., one that is weak and, consequently, either skinny or obese). Male beauty, then, is not only "handsome"—proportionate, symmetrical, developed through some physical training—it also is manifest in the union of a disciplined body and a disciplined mind, which creates or manifests a calm spirit. It is the appearance of outer strength and calmness, which reflects a deep, cultivated inner strength and inner calmness. And just as the female dancer is more beautiful for maintaining a calm demeanor during the dance, so male beauty is especially noticeable in times of stress and is expressed as reassurance, confidence, and concern for and loyalty to others. These are the qualities that we must cultivate.

I encourage you to think about beauty and aesthetics in your own life. See how you are uplifted by beauty, whether that is human beauty or a beautiful landscape or building. To use Gurdjieff's term, appearance is a mood-altering "food." If we live in a place that is dirty, noisy, and crowded, we will likely become angry or anxious. If we live in a place that is clean, neat, and close to nature and we are with close friends and family, we will be more likely to feel calm. Consider aesthetics in regard to your own home as well as your own clothing. A tidy home or office will enable you to think more clearly. But we are speaking of something beyond that. Consider things aesthetically. Create an environment that uplifts and nourishes your soul.

10

TECHNOLOGICAL NOISE AND INNER SILENCE

"SILENCE, ACCORDING TO WESTERN AND EASTERN TRADITION alike," observed philosopher and Catholic priest Ivan Illich, "is necessary for the emergence of persons." Only with periods of silence and with space to contemplate can we really begin to know ourselves. Ancient and classical cultures knew this. In traditional art, in scenes of dehumanization, there are rarely just one or two people depicted. Rather, scenes of dehumanization depict crowds.

As in medieval paintings of hell and in the fine art of World Wars I and II, the figures are usually crowded on top of each other. In these works, there is no privacy and no dialogue. They are scenes of noise— human, architectural, and machine noise. In English artist Christopher R. W. Nevinson's black-and-white etching *A Dawn* (1914), infantrymen are crowded into a street. They are pressed up against the walls and packed tightly together; we see only their heads, shoulders, swords, and the tops of their backpacks. Every soldier is identical to every other soldier, and each—his features sharp and angular like the sword and the buildings—is a machine for killing. Likewise, from the other side of the war, in his etching *Sturmtruppe geht unter Gas vor* (Stormtroopers advance under gas attack), German artist Otto Dix depicts soldiers packed together in a landscape destroyed by bombs. Each soldier has been rendered anonymous by a white gas mask strongly reminiscent of a human skull.

But we can step outside of war conflict to scenes of ordinary life to see the same dehumanization and the same crowds. In William Hogarth's etching *Gin Lane* (1751), crowds are hemmed in by buildings, their corners sharply dissecting the cityscape. A mob is shouting. A man gnaws on a bone. In the distance, a body is being placed into a coffin, but the crowd is too preoccupied and too busy to notice. Only some stone steps offer any space, and on them is slumped a woman so inebriated that she has let her baby slip from her arms to fall to its death. A few steps down a man has collapsed. He is unconscious from drinking gin, his eyes are closed, and his face and torso are skeletal. He has fed his addiction and starved himself.

Closer to our own time, in a painting called *The Crowd* (circa 1915), Wyndham Lewis depicted a modern city such as we might find in Tokyo or New York City today (but which did not exist at that time). High-rise buildings made of steel girders, concrete, and glass tightly pack the city. There are no trees, and we cannot even see the sky. In some of the buildings' windows are people working (much as we would see in any office block today) or perhaps gazing outside. Others are walking along the street. And here and there, crowds are rioting or protesting. But none of the figures is really fully human. Lewis—a misanthropist, bigot, critic, and founder of the short-lived Vorticist art movement—has recreated the human being to make it appear mechanical: its face is featureless and its limbs have the appearance of small girders or bits of scrap metal that could not be used for scaffolding. What matters in

Lewis's world is the technology—technology that would dominate and expel anything natural or traditional.

An essential element in conveying a sense of the spiritual is space. It is true, of course, that we sometimes do see numerous figures in religious art, but they are often neatly organized around a central figure, such as Jesus or the Buddha, and they are often saints or supernatural beings, such as angels, who emit light. In some scenes of the crucifixion of Christ, we sometimes find a crowd of onlookers and gawkers, some of them hostile to Jesus. But the crucified Christ and, on either side of him, the crucified thieves draw our eyes upward, away from the crowd. And suspended above the people below, the crucified figures are often set against a background of an empty sky or perhaps solid gold leaf. We are taken from crowdedness to emptiness, from noise to silence, from the material world to the sacred.

Not all premodern depictions of space or emptiness are religious, though most of them suggest something spiritual or sacred. During the Song dynasty, the Chinese painter Ma Yuan developed the "one-corner" composition of painting that concentrated most of the details in—as the name suggests—one corner of the paper, leaving most of the paper blank. However, "blank" isn't really the right term. The imagination naturally transforms the blankness into something else. A tree and some grass in the corner makes the empty paper appear as mist, obscuring some landscape behind it. And a small boat makes it appear as ocean water. But beyond the suggested landscape or ocean, there is a sense of the vastness of nature and of the Tao.

In the cathedral, synagogue, mosque, or temple, we also find incredible space. Most other buildings are designed around the proportions of the human body. Doors are a few inches taller than the human head. Ceilings are a foot or so above that. And windows are positioned so that, whether we are seated or standing, we can see outside. But the more impressive religious buildings were designed to house the spirit. And they are incomparably larger than those built to house the body. The door might be two or three times as tall as the average person, and windows might be positioned high up. (The ceiling of the Sistine Chapel is well over sixty feet high.)

Before they were dwarfed by commercial buildings, these religious edifices were usually the largest in any city (and in the West, cities were usually defined by the presence of a cathedral). Today, as corporations and architects vie to erect the tallest or most distinct buildings, it is easy for us to think that the height of the religious building was reflective of a desire for human power. And perhaps, partly it was. But walk into such a building and you will be reminded of the vastness of the cosmos or the vastness of space and, with that, the vastness of God or of what is beyond material existence and everyday concern.

We need to be reminded because it is a peculiar trait of the human being that we get used to and eventually almost cannot see or experience what is beautiful or miraculous. How many of us marvel at the night sky, with its distant stars, night after night? Almost none of us. How many of us really look at flowers or birds and find ourselves captivated by something wondrous? How many of us even really taste the food we eat? Or can even really focus our attention on being with the person we are with?

The cathedral, synagogue, mosque, or temple reminds us of the wonder of creation* and of the Creator. It is a place to go to remember

---

*On the facades of many older British churches can be found a "green man" figure, depicted as a male human head with leaves for skin and with leaves issuing from his mouth. It has been associated both with the pre-Christian "nature religions" and with the Christian notion of the Word of God.

the wonder that we once felt when looking at the stars* or at nature. When we experience a sense of wonder, we experience space and silence. We become totally absorbed in the thing that is making us feel wonder. Whatever is going on around us becomes unimportant, and our everyday concerns, our anger, jealousy, and pettiness, no longer exist.

The experience of nature—untransformed into concrete and glass zones and uncrowded by anonymous human beings—is integral to the human experience. It is, in fact, the world that we were designed for or evolved to live in. Quiet is a part of that experience. Of course, there is the sound of birds, cows, bees buzzing, the wind, rain, and so on. But there is not the incessant chatter of the human voice or technology.

In his "Silence Is a Commons" talk in 1983, Illich spoke of silence being broken by the introduction of the loudspeaker. In 1926, a month after he was born, he was taken to visit his grandfather on the island of Brac on the Dalmatian coast. His grandfather's house had been the family home for five hundred years. During that time, the island was ruled by different powers—the Ottoman empire, Venice, and Austria. Yet life itself had changed very little on the island. The same vats were being used to press wine. The same kind of boats were used for fishing. And olives were still being picked from the same olive trees.

But on the same boat that had taken Illich to the island, someone had brought a loudspeaker. Until then, said Illich, the people of Brac had spoken with similar strength. Now, however, natural quiet was no longer something enjoyed by all, more or less equally, but was competed over by those who possessed a microphone and who could amplify their voices over the natural voices of the people of Brac. There was no lon-

---

*In Masonic lodge buildings, the ceilings are very often painted to represent the starry night sky.

ger silence as such. Rather, if you did not own a loudspeaker, you were "silenced," natural quiet being transformed into impotence by the threat of the amplifying machine.

For Illich, the loudspeaker, which had so violently broken into the quiet, disturbing the community and customs of Brac, signified the beginning of a trend that was, by then, threatening to spread across the world. Already, increasingly, "electronic devices and systems" were taking over human life, rendering it in some way nonhuman. And silence, in particular, was being taken from people "by machines that ape people" and yet that made the human being more machinelike.

Illich was prophetic in his concern that we might even "be made increasingly dependent on machines for speaking and for thinking, as we are already dependent on machines for moving."[1] But he was far from the first person to notice the trajectory of technology. We have already made reference to Lewis's depiction of the modern city. And we have noted the dehumanization of the soldier in modern warfare.

Having fought in World War I, Ernst Jünger published his diary—a frank and unapologetic description of armed conflict—under the title *In Stahlgewittern* (Storm of steel). It quickly became the bible of former soldiers of the German army and within a few years had been translated into French, English, and other European languages. Although he was acutely aware of the horrors of mechanized warfare, Jünger had been struck, in 1912, two years before the outbreak of the world war, by the sinking of the luxury passenger liner the *Titanic* and by technology's potential to unexpectedly unleash death and disaster.

Although it is, and was, obvious that the technology of war would be used to kill and injure, what impressed itself so forcefully on Jünger was that with the sinking of the *Titanic,* there collided "the hubris of progress with panic" and "the highest comfort with destruction."[2]

Writing a few years after World War II and in response to Nazi and Soviet totalitarianism, Jünger suggested that the sinking of the *Titanic* had been a "turning point," at least in the psyche of his fellow countrymen. Fear had become symptomatic of the time, and fear, he suggested, was linked to the "growing automatism."

Introduced as a time-saver or as a luxury, technology often quickly turns into a necessity. Today, we must have a phone and an email account to apply for even the lowest-paid job. But especially higher up the career ladder, it's also necessary for us to keep up with technology itself and to display to those around us that we are keeping pace. We cannot have just any phone that works, but rather we must have the latest model. The same applies to everything from our computer to our food processor.

Like Illich more than three decades later, Jünger claimed that "man restricts his own power of decision in favor of technological expediencies."[3] Jünger—a soldier and author—would probably be shocked, but not entirely surprised, to see the degree to which we have become dependent on technology, especially to do the thinking for us. Instead of reading deeply to practice the art of contemplation, the contemporary individual skims articles or watches videos, not formulating his own opinions but absorbing them from carefully selected "experts" through a kind of technological osmosis. Rudderless in the world and not having any philosophy, religion, or worldview to guide him, he changes his convictions as the opinions of the experts change. Although he does not realize it, he is in a state of hypnosis.

But it is not only his decision-making power that contemporary man has surrendered. He does not imagine or daydream, but watches a movie instead. (And over the decades, his capacity for creativity wanes.)[4] He does not enjoy silence but seeks constant distraction instead—

music, a video, a movie, an instant chat, a comment on social media to argue over anonymously, an article to skim, and so on. (Anything to block out the doubts and thoughts in his head.) He cannot or does not want to escape the distraction. His technology goes everywhere with him, counting how many steps he has taken, how many calories he has burned, making him accessible to anyone no matter where he is, tracking him, beeping and buzzing, and alerting him to every "update."

Writing in the middle of the twentieth century, Josef Pieper noted that our conception of work had already grown "to cover and include the whole of human activity and even of human life."[5] Pieper asked, "Is there a sphere of human activity, one might even say of human existence, that does not need to be justified by inclusion in a five-year plan and its technical organization?"[6] As Pieper knew, for the modern individual, the answer is *no*. Yet historically, he notes, the *artes serviles* (servile arts or ordinary work) were distinct from the *artes liberales* (liberal arts).[7] Understanding itself was divided into both *ratio* and *intellectus*. Ratio is the rational—examination, logical thought, and deduction. It is work. Intellectus is contemplation and, being receptive, is not work.[8] We experience intellectus in looking at the rose, for example. "Our soul is passive and receptive."[9] We become absorbed in it. We experience gnosis.*

Earlier, we noted that in his celestial form, Krishna's eyes are said to be the sun and moon. And we also said that this must have suggested to ancient man that the celestial body of the Godhead was so vast as to be beyond human comprehension. Today in the West we would tend to explain these celestial eyes of Krishna as symbolizing the masculine (the sun) and the feminine (the moon), and we might liken them to the Taoist yin and yang or the Tibetan dual entity Yab-Yum (the

---

Gnosis is the Greek word for "knowledge," generally used to refer to direct knowledge of God (Arabic: *ma'rifa*).

father-mother). Perhaps we might even legitimately make such a comparison, but the price we pay is that we see things using only ratio, not intellectus. We place ourselves outside of the phenomenon to compare and examine it and think we have understood it. Defaulting to skepticism, intellectualization, and criticism, it is very hard for the contemporary individual to actually experience.

To truly experience, we have to cultivate inner silence. We have spoken about positive thinking, breathing, meditation, and prayer, all of which can give us calmness and focus. But inner silence is intellectus, the contemplation of something or being absorbed by something that is in the world outside of us. To experience this, we have to turn off technology for a time, and we have to be inaccessible to others for a time. We need to have a time when we aren't productive but in which insights have a chance of appearing to us—a time to be absorbed by the sight of a cloud, a bird, a tree, an old building, or a painting. We have to really contemplate it, not comparing it to the cloud, bird, or painting we saw somewhere else, but just finding what is beautiful, even miraculous, in what is before us right now. To cultivate inner silence is to accept that our own inner chatter, our inner noise, is very weak in the face of reality.

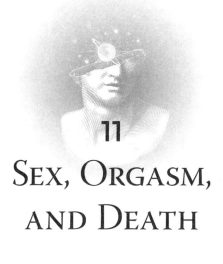

11

SEX, ORGASM, AND DEATH

IN MANY IMPORTANT RESPECTS, Sir Gawain's world is absolutely unlike ours. Not only are the forests through which he must travel so greatly reduced in size and our contact with the wilds so incredibly limited, but as writer and philosopher Colin Wilson has noted, the modern individual feels a sense of "insignificance." And he feels that insignificance when he compares himself with the mass of the population of his country,[1] which in nearly all cases run into the tens or hundreds of millions of people. Out in the wilds, which in some places are still large enough to dwarf him, the landscape, the stars, the sun, and moon open him up to the cosmos and to the Creator—or to belief in a Creator—to which he is somehow connected. Yet the mass of people presses down on us, psychologically. It is each of us against everyone else. Even romantic relationships can seem adversarial or transactional. There appears to be nothing worth sacrificing ourselves for or to. This is the tragedy of modern man: there seems nothing worth dying for and, thus nothing worth living for.

Man has always been attracted to greatness, vastness, glory, and ecstasy. He wants no half measure. He wants the extreme. "Thou art neither cold nor hot. . . . So then because thou art lukewarm . . . I will spue thee out of my mouth," reads Revelation (3:15–16). The heroic man sets out to conquer an overwhelming enemy, to climb the tallest mountain, to reach the North or South Pole or the moon before anyone else. Now he looks to Mars. But the contrary is also true. Men fighting in war to defeat a hated enemy have been prepared to die or to suffer for their comrades. In the story of *Sir Gawain and the Green Knight,* Gawain himself offers to face the Green Knight not because he is eager to prove himself or to kill the stranger but because his comrades appear afraid and unwilling and because someone must accept the challenge, like it or not. Man wants to conquer nature but also to be conquered by it and be changed by it.

Self-sacrifice is part of the heroic personality, and what the heroic or fully actualized individual is seeking is to immerse himself in what is greater than himself. The insignificance that the contemporary individual feels when he compares himself with the mass of the population is crushing. We want the opposite. Not a sense of our own importance, but a sense of belonging to something profound and meaningful—transcendent, even—that will outlast us. Glory in battle might be one way in which man achieves this. In every premodern culture, the great warrior and the great victory were sung or spoken of in tales for generations. But glory is merely one expression of it. We find it, too, in ecstasy, wonder, and awe.

In the sexual experience—in orgasm—we experience ecstasy. In looking out into the vastness of nature—the canyon, the ocean, the forest, the starry sky—we experience a sense of wonder. And in thinking of the Creator or looking at religious imagery, we experience a sense of awe. As we have noted, the cathedral, with its high ceilings and scale that dwarfs man, makes us aware of not only the architectural marvel but also the vastness of creation itself. And of course, it is intended to.

In theory, just like the mass of the population that dwarfs us, the vast canyon, the starry sky, or the soaring cathedral also should make us feel insignificant. But they do not. Instead, they remind us that there is something beyond us, beyond the rational, beyond the everyday concerns, that there is a Mystery and perhaps a God or a transcendent Intelligence that we are in some way connected to. Nature does not dwarf us or press down on us but draws us out into it. We are captivated by the expanse and peer into it, wondering what it must be like.

Though unacknowledged by contemporary society, the romantic nature of men is unlike that of women. The romance of women is one of life (or what Freud called the "life drive," or Eros). It is expressed through flowers, dancing, candlelit dinners, Valentine's Day, and other things that don't interest most men. In fact, we have come to associate "romance" so closely with such ritual expressions of love and attraction that it is almost impossible for us to think of it as anything else. Yet as the Norse warrior who longed for death could have told us, the romance of men is one of death (or what Freud called the "death drive," Thanatos).

For the Norse warrior, there was no fate worse than dying peacefully in bed. He wanted to slaughter, yes, but he also wanted to be slaughtered, to be cut down in his prime, in a moment of heroic struggle. Then a beautiful maiden—a Valkyrie—would swoop down from the sky and take him to Valhalla, the hall of the slain, to fight, feast, and wait for the final battle in which the gods, their warriors, and their enemies would all be destroyed. Likewise, in Islam, it is generally believed that male Muslims who die in battle will be rewarded with paradise in which there will be beautiful and voluptuous female companions called houris.

There is a story associated with Islamic chivalry that illustrates the romantic role of death in the male psyche. Accordingly, one day, in the midst of battle, Ali—the "Lion of Allah"—was confronted by a handsome young warrior. Seeing him approach, sword in hand, and realizing how the young man would surely fail to kill him, Ali felt pity for the young man and called out to him, warning him that he would be killed if he continued his approach. Why, Ali asked, would he want that? The young man called back, saying that he had fallen in love with a young woman. She would be his if he succeeded in killing the Lion of Allah, she had promised. And if he died? There could be no better reason to die than for love, the young man said, and at least he would be free of the lovesickness he felt. Moved by his words, Ali let his sword fall to the ground, took off his helmet, and exposed his neck, sacrificing himself to the young man. But upon seeing Ali's actions, the young man's love for the woman was transferred to Ali and the Prophet of Islam.[2]

In this story, we have all the motifs of the male romantic nature: the beautiful woman, the battle, and the heroic acts of self-sacrifice. The woman is life, and the man willingly sacrifices his for her because in dying or risking death he finds purpose and meaning—he finds life itself. It is an almost religious act (and in the above story the self-sacrifice ends in religious conversion). Yet the desire to die for a woman presents an existential riddle to the warrior. If he succeeds in this task, he will be dead and she will be alive and, of course, available to other men. The myths of the Valkyries and the houris solve that riddle by revealing the existence of a woman or women of extraordinary beauty who are available only to those who die in battle.

Unsurprisingly, girls and women have typically been celebrated at and elaborately adorned for weddings and festivals of fertility, beauty, or the goddess (hence, the May Queen and, to a certain extent, the modern beauty pageant). Men, in contrast, have typically been "decorated" in relation to violence and defense, whether real or ritually acted; hence, the medals worn by the soldier, contemporary gang colors, tribal tattoos, war paint, and some fraternal regalia (such as the triangular black apron adorned with a skull and crossbones at its center worn by members of the chivalric Masonic Order of the Temple).

Women are also given flowers as a celebration of their beauty or youthfulness or as an expression of personal love. Men are given flowers, often in a collective act, after a heroic death. Consider the Spanish festival of Las Mayas, in which girls between seven and eleven years of age are dressed in floral crowns and sit on an altar surrounded by elaborate floral displays while musicians sing of their beauty. Contrast this with Remembrance Day or Poppy Day (November 11 each year),* in Britain, Canada, Australia, and New Zealand, during which wreaths of red poppies are publicly laid on the Tomb of the Unknown Soldier. (The soldier was designated as "unknown" because the condition of his body made it impossible to identify who he was in life or to even know his nationality.)

Poppies were one of the few flowers to grow in war-torn Belgium during World War I, where much of the fighting took place. Although, with their hole-like black center and blood-red petals, the flowers are evocative of a bullet wound, the war and its atrocities became increasingly associated with the poppy after the publication of the poem "In Flanders Fields" (1915) by Canadian army physician John McCrae. The poem opens,

> *In Flanders fields the poppies blow*
> *Between the crosses, row on row.*

---

*In the United States, a lesser-known National Poppy Day is commemorated on May 24 in recognition of American troops who fought in World War I.

The female is life and celebrated as life. She is beauty, fertility, the mother. The male is death. He brings death. He dies. And occasionally, he gives voice to the slaughtered, sometimes in savage acts of revenge and sometimes in poetry. "We are the Dead," McCrae's poem eerily proclaims, though a few days ago we "loved and were loved."

Let us not fool ourselves; young men often dream about battle, sometimes imagining themselves as part of a small group of comrades achieving victory against all odds. At other times, though, the young man imagines dying in battle or dying in the arms of a lover, having performed some heroic act. While, doubtlessly, many men lose their dreams in the doldrums of routine, the heroic man—or the romantic man—does not. What he seeks is to conquer and to be conquered. The mountaineer wants to conquer the mountain, but he also wants to look out across an unforgiving and inhospitable landscape where man cannot exist for long, to see the colossal and primordial-like expanse of ice and rock and to lose himself in it, never to be the same again. Or he dreams of being mystically absorbed into Mother Nature or into God, or of experiencing an ego-destroying bliss—the *petite mort* infinitely extended—in an act of sex.

It is true, as Camille Paglia has said, that for a man, the sexual act necessarily ends in a "flop."[3] But the self-defeat—the fall that follows the rise—is problematic not for occurring but for the demise not being extreme enough. It is a surrender—exhaustion, not death. As the Norse warrior wants to die in battle and the mountaineer seeks to overwhelm himself with a sense of awe at nature, so the healthy man wants to meet his equal—or more than his equal—during sex, to be brought to both the dizzy height and the edge of consciousness, where there is only the vast sky all around and certain death below. Hence, Nike, the winged and often seminaked goddess of victory of ancient Greece, the winged and naked goddess Ishtar, the Valkyrie who descends from the sky to take the dead to Valhalla, or the ancient Egyptian goddess Nuit, whose body of deep blue sky and stars suspends itself over the smaller but sometimes erect, green body of Geb, the earth god; hence, too, the popular Dungeons and Dragons–style image of the succubus with bat's wings. And such modern depictions of the strong, sexually alluring woman as Trinity, the gun-toting martial arts adept in tight, black spandex of *The Matrix* movies; the scantily clad, sword-wielding Xena in *Xena: Warrior Princess;* or the similarly impractically dressed Wonder Woman.

In sex, the strong male wants to lose himself, to invoke and embody his daemon, and in the act of sex, he wants to entice and provoke his lover to transform into the wrathful, all-devouring dark goddess and to slay him. In her, in the moment of ecstasy, he wants to look on the face of an anima that is both the Creator and the Destroyer. It is no coincidence that in traditional depictions of the Hindu goddess Kali, she dangles a severed male head from one of her hands. Or that in some Tantric imagery, Kali is depicted standing on the corpse of the god Siva (whose erect member points directly up between the legs of the goddess) while she dangles a severed male head over his.*

And it should come as no surprise that the decapitation of the male body has been a theme of importance in Western painting as well, where it is often tinged with the erotic and the mystical. Judith beheading

---

*In one ancient Egyptian myth, the god Osiris is killed and later dismembered by his brother Seth. The goddess Isis turns herself into a bird and searches across the land for Osiris. Then she puts his body back together, uses her magic to bring him back to life temporarily, and copulates with the god. In some accounts, Osiris's penis is missing, but Isis uses her magic to make the body of Osiris whole. And although this story is not sexual in nature, in Norse mythology, the god Odin receives wise counsel from the severed head of the giant Mimir.

Holofernes has been portrayed by artists including Michelangelo, Sandro Botticelli, and Gustav Klimt. The tale from the deuterocanonical book of Judith describes how Judith enters the tent of the Assyrian general Holofernes, who is intent on destroying her hometown, Bethulia. She is able to visit the general because she is beautiful and because he desires her. Once he has passed out from drink, she beheads the general to save her people.

Unsurprisingly, just as Kali is portrayed as voluptuous though terrifying, in Western fine art Judith is often portrayed naked or seminaked. In Franz von Stuck's 1928 painting *Judith,* she stands naked and fully exposed to the viewer, hovering over the body of the general, sword in hand, about to decapitate him. In Klimt's 1901 painting *Judith and the Head of Holofernes,* we see a dark-haired woman from the navel up, naked except for a sheer garment with a gold pattern. She holds the head of Holofernes to the side, at waist height. Around her head (which is symbolically separated or distinguished from the torso by a large gold choker) is a scalelike pattern and trees, all in gold. If you look at her from the neck up, Judith appears to be immersed in the dreamlike, the ecstatic, and, possibly, the orgasmic. Last, in Cornelis Galle the Elder's 1610 etching on this theme, Judith is in the midst of beheading the general. His eyes have rolled back slightly, and his mouth is open. As blood spurts from his neck, beams of light pour in from above, and cherubs hover over the scene. There is death but also, possibly, ecstasy.

Again, Salome holding (and sometimes kissing) the severed head of John the Baptist has been celebrated in Western art by Bernardino Luini, Gustave Moreau, and Henri Regnault, among many other male artists. In 1906, Franz von Stuck painted three very similar versions of Salome. Highly sexual, in these the femme fatale is shown naked from the waist up (except for jewelry), her head thrown back, and her right arm raised in such a way that it is reminiscent of a Spanish dancer. Grinning, Salome appears enraptured and thrilled by the saint's death. In von Stuck's depictions, it is a servant who holds the head, though he fades into the background—a star-studded night sky—while the head of the saint is aglow with a halo.

The night sky is a significant motif here. Visually, the dark, starry night sky frames the pale, naked torso. Since nothing else is shown around Salome or her servant, the whole of the drama appears to be taking place in this cosmic space, and although her head is thrown back in delight, it is nonetheless turned toward the sky and the stars. In regard to what that might signify, it suggests a consciousness beyond man's— the consciousness of the Creator or of the Tao, which man can perhaps merge with if he can halt the endless stream of thoughts and empty his mind. Ultimately, everything is going on in a cosmic, or a divine, realm that is beyond our physical nature and that will affect us after death.

In Tantra, this is represented by a form of the goddess called Chhinnamasta. When she is depicted, she is shown naked except for a garland of severed human male heads. Her own head is severed, and— still alive—she holds it in her left hand and drinks her own blood. Usually, she is shown standing on the bodies of a naked man and woman, who are copulating (representing the union of the energies of the body). Chhinnamasta signifies the consciousness that has left the body and the consciousness of ratio behind, having been dissolved into "pure awareness."[4]

Although there is nothing evidently sexual about Aubrey Beardsley's celebrated 1893 depiction of Salome, the title of the work—*The Climax*— suggests a connection to the sexual act. In it, Salome floats above the ground, perhaps like a witch, holding the head of the saint and staring intensely into its eyes. The head signifies the ego—the "I" consciousness that sees itself as separate to everything else and that must be killed if we are to reach enlightenment. The orgasm—the petite mort—is "the little death," but we yearn for a great death, if not in the literal sense, then in the sense signified by the head held by Kali or in the sense represented by the Death tarot card: total transformation, death and rebirth, a step into the great unknown, the abyss, and into bliss.

In *Sir Gawain and the Green Knight*, the Green Knight himself is beheaded and, like the goddess Chhinnamasta, the decapitated knight holds his own severed head up for everyone to see. Gawain must believe that he himself will soon be decapitated and that, unlike the Green Knight, he will obviously not survive it. And notably, as his journey begins to draw to a close and the time to face the ax draws near, sex— or, at least, sexual temptation—enters the picture.

After nearly a whole year of traveling alone, Gawain comes across a castle and, after asking for shelter, is invited in. A feast is held for the knight. There is celebration and laughter, but Gawain tells the lord of the castle that he must depart. Upon hearing that the knight is seeking the Green Chapel, the lord insists that Gawain stay and rest, and since it is close by, he promises to show Gawain how to get there in a few days' time. While Gawain is resting, the lord will go out hunting. This sounds easy enough. But the lord then makes an unusual bargain with Gawain. Whatever he wins in the hunt each day, he will give to Gawain, but whatever the knight wins in the castle, he will give to the lord.[5]

The following morning, while the lord is out hunting, his wife enters Gawain's chamber and attempts to seduce him.[6] Although there are, of course, exceptions, in general, men have a stronger libido than women and think about sex more often than women.[7] And because men are typically attracted to a woman's looks and charm (and don't usually care about her ability to earn an income, for example), sex is a perennial temptation for men, regardless of their status in society or personal circumstances (hence, the sex scandals of so many politicians and more than a few religious leaders). Yet Gawain has four things that can enable men to take a step back: loyalty, honor, a sense of mission, and the recognition of his mortality.

We will look at loyalty again in a moment. Here, we should note that not sleeping with the wives or girlfriends of one's compatriots is almost always a spoken or unspoken code within male societies. It would cause too much trouble within the group and could tear it apart. In some male societies (such as gangs), it might lead to the severe physical punishment of the offender. And while such behavior might be seen as a mark of prowess or manliness in the general society (or perhaps even as an act of naked but mutual lust), within the all-male group, it will be viewed as an act of sneakiness; underhandedness; disloyalty; and, when going behind the backs of the other men, even as an act of unmanliness. Indeed, it is a weak man who flirts with his friends' girlfriends and hits on every woman who floats across his horizon.

Loyalty is often related to honor and is sometimes synonymous with it. However, while loyalty is dedication to the group (and can remain even if the group becomes corrupt), honor is dedication to the highest ideals of the group. And an individual with a sense of honor exemplifies the highest ideals even when he is away from other members of the group. Should the group become corrupt—abandoning its values for convenience, prestige, or money—though the loyal members will remain (often vying for positions of power and influence), the most honorable members might find themselves in active opposition to it.

A sense of mission can also help men from being sidetracked by sexual desire. If a man feels that he must work hard to overcome some weakness in himself, to become all that he is capable of, or that he has work to do that will affect not just himself but also his community, his tribe, or his gang, or if he feels that there is some destiny that he must fulfill, he will be able to go without the normal distractions—bars, late nights out, casual sex, junk food, and junk entertainment. It is his sacrificing of comfort that distinguishes a man's sense of mission from the more common "sense of purpose." Yet a sense of mission is often related to a sense of mortality. He recognizes that time is short and that he will inevitably die. If he is to shape the future or if his name is to be remembered (a common concern among ancient peoples), he must act now. In Greek mythology, Jason had himself bound to the mast of his ship so that he would be forced to resist the temptation of the Sirens. He was on a mission to obtain the Golden Fleece. Gawain's mission is to reach the Green Chapel, where he has to face the ax of the Green Knight.

When the lord's wife enters Gawain's chamber, the knight pretends to be asleep, but he is unable to fool her, and he begins to banter with the lady and—with her persisting—finally accepts to kiss her. This, he says, is befitting of a knight, but he will do no more. Upon his return, the lord orders his staff to assemble in the hall, and he presents Gawain with the best meat cut from the ribs of the animal his party had killed and then demands from the knight whatever he has won in the castle. True to his word, Gawain kisses the lord.[8] The next day follows in much the same way. Again, the lady attempts to seduce Gawain; again, he gives her no more than a kiss; and again, the lord brings meat for his guest and, in return, demands what his guest had won.[9] On the third day, however, the lady gives Gawain a green belt, which, she says, protects the wearer and makes him impossible to kill. And believing that the Green Knight intends to kill him, the young knight keeps it for himself.

There is a clear relationship between the lady's tempting of Gawain and the lord's hunts. Described in lengthy and graphic detail, the killing and dismemberment of the animals, which take place at the same time as the attempted seductions, make it clear that hunting is a craft of death, just as the lady's actions represent a craft of life because her success would likely lead to pregnancy. But there is more to it than subtly juxtaposing death and sex. On the first day, the hunting party allows the stags and bucks (male) to go free[10] but slaughters a (female) deer.[11] The male deers escape death just as Gawain escapes the attempted seduction (which we learn much later in the story would have led to his being killed, though not by the lady). The following day, the party hunts down a fierce wild boar[12] (an animal associated with strength), and in her attempt to seduce Gawain, the lady remarks on and seems preoccupied with his physical strength.[13] On the third day, when Gawain takes the lady's green belt, believing it will protect him through occult or magical power, the lord and his hunting party chase and kill a fox, an animal associated with cunning and deviousness. Though taking the belt is not strictly against the pacts that Sir Gawain made with the Green Knight and the lord of the castle, it is clearly against their spirit and could easily have been seen as underhand and sneaky.

What occurs in the wilds outside the castle reflects what goes on inside the castle. This is not a mere literary device of a medieval poet. The mind and actions of Sir Gawain and the lady affect the outcome of the hunt. And the hunt thus is a kind of divinatory reading that reveals what is taking place in the castle. Because Gawain chooses to accept the aid of magic, a fox is killed. And because the lady fails in her seduction, a female deer, specifically, is killed and the stag let free.*

---

*In the Volsunga Saga, Gudrun dreams that she captures a large, male deer with golden hair that is then slaughtered by Brynhild. This foretells the marriage of Gudrun to Sigurd and the death of the latter. See Jesse L. Byock, *The Saga of the Volsungs: The Norse Epic of Sigurd the Dragon Slayer*, 77.

Had they acted differently, different animals would have been killed.

Gawain and the lady embody the archetypal, and, as such, they are connected to and are a part of the archetypal as it appears throughout nature. They embody the male and female not only in animal nature but also as it is embodied throughout the cosmos—in the sun god and moon goddess, in the ancient Egyptian sky goddess Nuit and earth god Geb, in the Tibetan Tantric Yab-Yum (father-mother), in the yin (female) and yang (male) of Taoism, and so on. Together, the male and female embody a kind of supermind, a spiritual and cosmic force or, to borrow Napoleon Hill's term, "infinite intelligence."

The perception of nature as a kaleidoscope of male and female forms is found especially among ancient and so-called primitive societies, where we find not only the sun and moon but also each aspect of nature conceived of as one (or, rarely, both) of the sexes. Even rocks, according to their shape, can be thought of as male or female—a reflection of which we find in the Hindu Siva linga.* Tools, likewise, were thought of as either male or female (e.g., the hammer and anvil). Although much later in time, the Latin term *vagina* referred to a sword's sheath while the term for a sword (*gladius*) could also refer to the penis, and long after the blacksmith has disappeared from daily life, there is still a British slang expression, "going at it, hammer and tongs," which refers to vigorous sexual intercourse between a man and a woman.

The tale presents Gawain's encounter with the woman as his successfully remaining chaste despite temptation. Though he breaks his word when he keeps the belt, Gawain refuses the lady because he wants

---

*The Siva linga (representing the male generative power) is usually placed into a yoni (signifying the cosmic womb, vagina, or origin). Nevertheless, the Siva linga is also sometimes regarded as the cosmic egg. See Mookerjie and Khanna, *The Tantric Way: Art, Science, Ritual,* 45.

to keep his word to the lord. The ability to say *no* is essential if we want to say *yes* to achieving anything meaningful. To focus on what gives our life purpose and value, we must say *no* to those people and activities that will waste our time. Often, at a crucial moment in our work, we will be offered an "escape" from our work for a few hours—socializing, drinking, or some kind of entertainment. At other times, we will be offered a project or a position that does not suit us but that we might feel obliged to take either because of financial reward or because a friend has offered it to us (perhaps for no financial compensation).

There is something else in Gawain's rejection of the woman's sexual advances. In Tantric and Taoist inner alchemy, instead of being released, semen—being considered a congealed, material form of a universal energy—is transmuted and redirected so that the practitioner creates an immortal energy body. On a more earthly note, while the negative effect of sex on performance in other activities has been questioned, anyone who trains physically will realize that sex can be both distracting and depleting of mental energy.[14] The focus does not appear to be as sharp. The body feels softer. Indeed, leaving modern science aside, the depletion of energy in men has long been observed. Abu Bakr Muhammad ibn Zakariya al-Razi suggested that too much sexual intercourse not only reduced the individual's strength but also would make him age prematurely.[15]

Psychologically, for men, sex is linked to status and reward. We celebrate a victory with sex. If we want more sex, we must be victorious more often, improve ourselves in some way, and raise our stature among the men and women in our society or our in-group. We must be a "winner." Whether we like it or not, while women are judged primarily on their looks, men are generally judged only partly on their physical appearance and partly on their status, self-confidence, intellect, ability to earn a living, and so on. There is no point is thinking that either men or women have it easier. You must make the best of your situation.

Throughout young manhood, especially, most men are constantly distracted by sexual desire. And men in their fifties have suddenly made a fortune because they are no longer preoccupied by sexual thoughts and desires, claims Napoleon Hill in *Think and Grow Rich*. Like the Taoist inner alchemist, he suggests that the sexual energy be redirected. But for Hill, this means focusing a man's time and energy on something other than the physical sexual act and, more specifically, on something that will benefit him in the world. If a man is sexually attracted to a woman and fantasizes about a life with her, Hill suggests, he might be inspired and energized to take action and to make his life more like that of his fantasies. Perhaps this will mean becoming an entrepreneur, making his body more muscular, or becoming more outgoing and confident. Whatever it is, he does it.[16]

As mentioned, Tantric and Taoist inner alchemy believe that semen—or its energetic essence—must not be released. Rather, it must be redirected within the body. Tantra explicitly speaks of redirecting semen to the brain. However, we must not take this literally. It is really a subtle life energy (what the Hindus call prana and what the Taoists call chi, or what the twentieth-century psychologist Wilhelm Reich called orgone) that is being spoken about. Such energy is present throughout the body and throughout the natural world. And it is particularly present in semen, which is needed to create new life.

Notably, the author of *Sir Gawain and the Green Knight* implies that there is some kind of energetic connection between man and nature. As soon as the Green Knight enters the story, we are aware that, like nature, he is green from head to foot. However, before he sets off on his journey, Gawain is dressed in the opposite color: red. His knight's shield is red.[17] His horse, Gringolet, is decked out in red and gold.[18] And his robe is red.[19] Red represents blood or animal life. Green represents sap or plant life. Nevertheless, while the Green Knight is green from head to foot, we are told that his eyes are red.[20] And Gawain, as we have seen, is given a green belt to wear. There is, in other words, a relationship between blood and sap, the animal and the vegetable kingdoms.

The author could not have known that the structure of hemoglobin is identical to that of chlorophyll (which gives plants their green color) except that the former has iron at its center and the latter magnesium. And as curious as this is, the connection between the blood and sap, man and nature, had been made by ancient man. The ancient Germanic tribes believed that the gods had made man and woman from an ash and an elm tree, and the Zoroastrians believed that man had been made from the rhubarb stalk. According to folklore, when a hanged man was on the gallows, he would spontaneously ejaculate at the moment of death and if his semen fell to the earth below, it would impregnate it, producing a mandrake plant. (The mandrake root has a humanlike shape to it and was said to scream when pulled out of the ground.) Last, there is the widespread phenomenon of the Green Man that is often carved in stone on older British churches and is depicted as a human male head made of leaves or with leaves issuing from his mouth. Human life and plant life are expressions of the same life energy—chi, prana, or orgone. And it is this universal energy that liquifies as blood and semen in man and as sap in plants.

We spoke earlier of the romantic nature of men being linked to death (and of the orgasm being the petite mort, or little death). We spoke of the actions of Gawain and the lady of the castle being reflected in the hunts of the lord and what animals were killed. And now we have found there to be a relationship between the energy of animal life and that of plant life—chi, prana, or orgone—and between blood and semen and sap. All of this suggests that we are connected to nature and to other living things through an energy that is itself joined to, and can be shaped by, consciousness or thoughts.

As we mentioned, Hill tells us that sexually stimulated, an individual can be inspired to create his own mission or to forge a new life. We want to have sexual desire and imagination. Sexual desire gives us energy. The mere sight of someone sexually attractive to us can shake us out of a depressed state and give us back a feeling of hope and the sense that we can decisively act in the world. But we also want the ability to contain and channel our sexual desires instead of being controlled by them.

We looked at the symbolism of the severed head earlier, and while the modern individual is inclined to associate the head with the intellect and to view the brain as a calculating machine, premodern man associated the head with the soul and the divine. The Buddha, Zarathustra, Jesus, saints, and other religious figures are often depicted with halos around their heads, not because they were regarded as clever but because they were believed to be either an embodiment of absolute reality or uniquely connected to it.

The severed head (which is so often accompanied by sexual suggestion or symbolism) represents the consciousness that has launched itself or that has been launched by the body from the consciousness *of the body*. It represents the higher, ecstatic consciousness—sexual or saintly—in which we experience gnosis, or knowledge of the divine. The orgasm is not only the petite mort, or little death; it also is the *petite gnosis*. The brain functions in a specific way during orgasm. The hypothalamus releases the "love hormone" oxytocin, the "pleasure chemical" dopamine is released, and the lateral orbitofrontal cortex— used in decision making—becomes less active. The orgasm is intense and nonrational. The mind spasms. There is an instantly fleeting void in the consciousness.

12

THE WARRIOR AND THE CREATIVE INDIVIDUAL

HAVING LEFT ARTHUR'S CASTLE A YEAR EARLIER, Gawain finally arrives at the Green Chapel. There, the Green Knight meets him and praises the young knight for fulfilling his obligation. Then the mysterious knight in green tells Gawain to hold still while he swings his ax at his neck. The first time, Gawain sees the ax coming toward him out of the corner of his eye and flinches. The ax misses his neck. The Green Knight tells him to be still and swings the ax a second time but does not kill or injure Gawain. Then, on the third swing, he cuts into the knight's neck. Blood spurts from the wound and onto the ground, though he is not seriously wounded.[1]

Just as the stag, boar, and fox are linked with Gawain's actions in the castle, so, too, are these blows, the Green Knight explains. It was his castle, he tells the young knight, and he had arranged for his wife to test him. Because Gawain had not given in to her sexual advances on the first or second day, the Green Knight had aimed the first and second blows of the ax so that they would miss Gawain's body. But because Gawain took the green belt on the third day, believing that it might save his life, the Green Knight grazed his neck with the third strike. It was dishonorable to accept the belt, which is the Green Knight's, and to try to cheat fate. But he understands that Gawain acted from momentary weakness and believes that it was not a serious transgression of the knightly code, especially as Gawain acknowledges his errors with a sense of remorse. Gawain is not perfect, but he strove to live up to his word, appearing at the Green Chapel as agreed and not allowing himself to be seduced by the lady of the castle.[2]

Cut off from society, the hero finds himself submerged in nature and, moreover, in supernatural or psychic communion with nature—or Nature, the primordial web of being. The hero has also had to face his own death, and he has had time to contemplate his mortality on his journey. The contemplation of mortality can be found in initiations and in religious practice alike. The samurai were supposed to contemplate dying in various unpleasant ways—by arrows, sword, or disease. The Buddhist might imagine his body dying and being reduced to bones. The Christian contemplates the crucifixion and, with that, faces his own mortality. In Freemasonry, as we have mentioned, the initiate to a lodge is sometimes asked to sit in the Chamber of Reflection and to contemplate his mortality. Such contemplations are not morbid, however. They are an attempt to reconcile the individual to the fact that his time on Earth is limited and that he must make the best of it, acting with integrity and striving to align himself with ultimate reality, the Tao, or with natural law, or dharma.

Today, the average individual doesn't contemplate death. It just doesn't strike him as real enough to think about. In 1998 the American Psychiatric Association claimed that by watching twenty-eight hours of television a week, the average American child would see sixteen thousand murders and two hundred thousand acts of violence portrayed by the time he or she was eighteen years old.[3] We might question those figures, but there is no doubt that death and violence are central to modern entertainment.

But precisely because it is entertainment and, perhaps, because we see the same actors being killed only to reappear in another movie or television drama, death and violence do not seem to be things that would ever happen to us. Indeed, how many people do you know who act as if they are somehow immune to being attacked? Or who openly say that that will never happen to them? Or who, with no self-defense training or real-life experience of violence, believe that they would be able to fend off even a much larger and more aggressive and experienced violent criminal with a single kick or punch? Their logic is that of the cartoon. Yet violence is quite real, and so, of course, is death.

Only in rare instances, when the government media continually warn of the threat of death (e.g., in the form of terrorism or a pandemic), do people take it seriously, though this often only stimulates unreasoned fear and a collective demand for more safety. Prior to the modern age, death was something experienced up close. Families had five, six, seven, perhaps even eight or nine children, partly because there was no contraception available to them and partly because at least some of the children would be dead well before they had a chance to reach adulthood. Children saw far fewer deaths than the modern individual, but those they saw were of real people—brothers, sisters, parents, grandparents, and neighbors. Death was personal, and with each one, part of the individual's world dropped away.

Men have always been aware of their mortality, although we are less so today. But in traditional societies, one's mortality has always been something *worth contemplating* and *worth remembering*. To reflect on one's limited time on Earth is to live differently. In traditional societies, that meant being obedient to God's law, or to the sharia, or to the dharma, or the Tao in life while looking forward to what might exist beyond the death of the material body. And as part of that, it also meant discovering one's own nature and embodying it. In less traditional societies, still, voluntarily facing one's mortality can spur extraordinary activity.

"He had the fatal speed of those who are to die young," wrote Arthur Symons about the artist Aubrey Beardsley.[4] Born in 1872, Beardsley came to prominence illustrating the work of Oscar Wilde as well as the scandalous *Yellow Book,* though his work would remain influential and inspired some artists of the hippie era of the 1960s and is still exhibited in museums today. Beardsley was prolific, but he was conscious that his time on Earth would be short and that he had no time to waste. At the age of six, he had contracted tuberculosis, for which there was then no known cure, and he died of the disease at just twenty-five, in 1898.

But Beardsley is hardly the only celebrity to have died young. Martial arts legend Bruce Lee died at thirty-two, Bob Marley at thirty-six, Vincent van Gogh at thirty-seven. Janis Joplin and Jim Morrison both died at twenty-seven. And having conquered territory from northwestern India and northeastern Africa, making his empire the largest the world had ever known, Alexander the Great died at thirty-two. These figures may not have thought that they would die so young, but as they were driven, innovative, visionary, and living their lives on the edge or over it, it is unlikely that they ever really envisioned growing old.

Civilizations, societies, and cultures also die. One reason for their decline is that the people lose conscious awareness of their mortality and thus can no longer take it seriously, and they cannot take anything seriously unless it impacts on their own sense of self-worth or their own identity. History and culture are forgotten when individuals become wrapped up in themselves—in their own egos—and begin to live as if there is neither a past nor a future but only an unending present or, worse, when they think that utopia is only a few acts of violence away.

In chapter 1 we looked at Ibn Khaldun's notion of the cyclical rise and fall of dynasties. To recap, Ibn Khaldun believed that dynasties went through three generations (which we described as three stages). In the first stage, warriors would conquer a senescent dynasty and, having conquered it, would rule while remaining true to the harsh desert values of the warrior. In the second stage, the people would live in relative luxury and would prefer the life of the city, though they would admire, and would secretly hope for a return of, the desert values. In the final stage, loving luxury and comfort, the people would become weak and would crave safety and protection. Sensing this weakness, a new band of warriors would take over the dynasty by force.

Civilizations can exist for a long time in denial of their decline, unaware that their spirit is seeping away. For Ibn Khaldun, it is the spirit of the warrior that the dynasty ultimately depends on, and the further through the three stages a dynasty advances, the more the warrior spirit recedes. However, for historian Arnold J. Toynbee, a civilization is kept alive, and occasionally revivified, by the "creative individual" (whom Toynbee also calls the "mystic") and by the "creative minority." For Toynbee, the "creative individual," or the "mystic" or visionary, goes through a specific process of "Withdrawal-and-Return."[5] First, he withdraws from the ordinary world—the world of "action"—into a world of "solitude," where he experiences "ecstasy" or receives a vision or revelation. (Think about our discussions on silence and sex.) Then, being transformed by the experience, the creative individual returns to the world with a new message. But there, says Toynbee, he must convert those of his civilization to his message because failure to do so will mean being ostracized or possibly even persecuted and destroyed.[6]

But the visionary can also cultivate or inspire a creative minority. And often with visionary thinkers, it is the direct students who carry the message into the world and make it accessible by stripping away the mystique and peculiar language in which it was originally formed and by expressing it in simpler, more accessible language. Or the ideas might seep into a society slowly, as if by one tiny drip at a time, until it has been transformed by them, even if the society is unaware of where its ideas came from. Indeed, most "civilized" people simply think that they believe what is true and do not realize that ideas have histories. Yet their convictions, and those of their society, are the haunted palaces of the dreams of dead philosophers—from Thomas Aquinas to Theodor Adorno and from al-Ghazali to al-Afghani—whom the majority cannot name.

Civilizations differ from "primitive" societies, says Toynbee, in that the latter are in a "static condition," whereas civilizations have a "dynamic movement," the engine of which is the creative minority.[7] Through mimicking the older generations and the dead of the tribe* (through ancestor worship, shamanic communion with the deceased, etc.) the "primitive society," claims Toynbee, preserves its customs, rules, rituals, myths, and way of life as if in amber, while, in contrast, the civilization—if it is not in decline—constantly revivifies and reinvents itself, largely through mimicking "the creative personalities that have broken new ground."[8]

The question for civilization, then, is always whether the new ground can sustain and perhaps even strengthen it over a long period of time or whether it is a mere dazzling distraction that might soon fade

---

*In our own time, the critic has taken on the role of the dead.

or that might—through some extreme political ideology that seeks to impose itself on others, perhaps especially on the most creative members of society—draw the civilization away from what can sustain it. "If aught I have said is truth," we read at the close of *The Prophet* of Kahlil Gibran, "that truth shall reveal itself in a clearer voice, and in words more kin to your thoughts." The purpose of Toynbee's creative individual must, ultimately, be to bring the truth back into the collective consciousness (i.e., to express a vision of life that is self-sustaining, healthy, strong, vigorous, aesthetic, and connected to the natural and the sacred) in an era in which the old vision no longer has an effect because conditions have changed so much that truth appears, to the general populace, to be old-fashioned and fails to inspire.

To slightly modify Toynbee's claim about the primitive society and civilization, we might say that in the former, the people listen to the elders and the dead of the tribe as a whole and, following their example and obeying their wishes, preserve the culture passed down to them as is. There is an egalitarian impulse. In the civilization—if it is not in decline but retains its dynamic movement—the cultural creators listen to those elders and deceased who were themselves creators (e.g., artists, composers, scientists, writers, and military strategists) and innovate so that the essence of the culture is brought forth for the new generation. They think through and beyond these ancestral creators, being inspired by their spirit rather than by a desire to reenact or to recite a corpus of rituals, rites, and texts. In a sense, regardless of the kind or size of the collective of which they are a part, the creative minority attempts to capture the dynamism of the moment that gave birth to the civilization and to use it as inspiration to continue the creative process. There is a creative and even an elitist impulse.

The creative minority—or the creative elite—sees itself as part of a vertical community, a cultural lightning flash that shoots out of the heavens and cuts through time, dispersing its energy outward to society itself. We find such vertical organizations not only in creative fields but also in religions. Hence, in Hinduism, the disciple meditates on his guru, who is seen as a link in a chain of gurus extending back through time. In Islam, Muhammad is regarded as the "seal of the prophets," which begins with Adam. And even in contemporary philosophy and art, the philosopher and the artist regard themselves as being in a lineage or as representing a continuation and reevaluation of those who shaped their respective fields.

The tribe that habitually and unquestioningly seeks to emulate its elders and dead exhibits a high degree of loyalty, as might the nihilist who wants to tear down society in the name of a particular class or group. But in being inspired by the cultural creators of the past, the creative minority has the possibility to return something akin to honor to the consciousness of the civilization. *Honor* is a curious word, perhaps. It is linked to the idea of acting honorably or living in a way that is uncompromised by others' corruption or by the temptation of financial gain or influence if one only bends one's sense of right and wrong. And yet, it is also linked to the idea of fame and renown and the receiving of "an honor" or an award for one's work or actions. While the creative individual may bring some new technology or art form to life, crucially, he also appears as an example of an uncompromising soul. He honors his ideal, and he honors those who have inspired him. (We noted in chapter 4 that Elon Musk had named his innovative car company Tesla after the inventor and scientific maverick Nikola Tesla.) And he receives honors from those who recognize his achievements.

The motto of the Prince of Wales is *Ich dien* (I serve). Despite its honor and nobility of spirit, the creative minority must recognize that it ultimately serves the ordinary people and serves generations yet unborn as much as, or more than, it serves itself. Rather than imposing itself on the people, the creative minority must remind each person of his or her true Self—of their own potential and their ability to defy their own weaknesses and fears. It must remind the people of the sacred, the healthy, strong, peaceful, and beautiful. And it must give them some method of elevating themselves in light of these qualities. (We have looked at many of these.)

To do this is to return to the simple. For no matter how dazzling its entertainment or technology, a society can stagnate and go out of balance. While Ibn Khaldun's warriors take over the decadent dynasty by force, speaking amorally, they also bring back the warrior spirit that had slowly seeped out of its culture, creating an imbalance. The warriors inadvertently initiate a new cycle because they are unable to unify the warrior spirit with the creative spirit and, as such, bring a new, although very different, type of imbalance.

Although both the warrior and the creative individual must be able to think nonrationally, thinking of possibilities not thought of before (the warrior so he can outmaneuver his enemy and the creative individual so that he can invent or design something new), they can only be united when they perceive themselves to be different expressions of the sacred. And the sacred ultimately means harmony: the harmony of body and mind, male and female, man and nature; the harmony of exercise, sleep, and diet; the harmony of color and form in art and architecture; and so on. Thus, in a society that is too masculine, the creative individual brings awareness of the divine feminine. And in a society too feminine, he brings awareness of the divine masculine. In a society that is too rational, the visionary brings a return of the nonrational, and vice versa. Likewise, if it has veered too far left or right, he aims to bring it back to the straight course—the "middle path," to borrow a phrase from Buddhism—and not to have it veer to the other extreme.

But in going against the tide that has swept up society, the creative individual will inevitably be regarded as an "immoralist."[9] When the momentum of a society has reached a certain velocity, it will be impossible for the majority to even conceive of a different way of acting or thinking, and even creativity itself will fall under suspicion. There are really only two paths open for the creative individual who finds himself in such a situation. Either he must embody a higher and stricter morality and nobler character than others, appearing unmoved by accusations and as a martyr to the few who are still able to perceive the dimming light of truth (and who might rally around him), or he must creatively indulge his desires, which also are desires in which the ordinary, morally outraged person wishes to indulge but is afraid to since he is unable to withstand the accusations and envy that he knows will result.

Hence, the creative individual is the Tantric priest of society. And in his creativity is a transcendent immorality. Because the people had become corrupt and "the earth was filled with violence," says the Bible, God sent a great flood to destroy mankind (Genesis 6:9–9:17). The flood myth appears in the story of Gilgamesh and in Plato's account of the destruction of Atlantis and elsewhere, of course. The Stoics also believed in a cyclical destruction by flood and by fire.

Less well known is the mythology recorded by the stonemasons' guild of Great Britain during the medieval period in what are now called the "Old Charges." In one of the earliest known of these texts (the Cooke Manuscript, circa 1450), it says that, fearing that God would destroy the world either by flood or fire, Tubal Cain (the inventor of metallurgy) and Namaah (the inventor of weaving) appealed to their elder brother Jabal (who had invented geometry and architecture) to make them two pillars, one that could withstand fire and the other that would be able to float on water, and to inscribe all of the "sciences" on them so that they would survive the catastrophe. There is no sense that these figures are in any way sinful, and presumably they are conscious of the impending destruction because they are aware that society has gone out of balance or that people have gone against their own natures. They are intent on preserving what is Godly—and what God has allowed man to discover—against the indiscriminate action of God. They are creators. In contrast, the populace, which has become corrupt and violent, has at the same time become the critic—the adversary—of God.

As Ibn Khaldun observed, civilizations rise and fall. In our own time, creativity is in decline. We expect to be able to purchase rather than to make, replace rather than fix, and react rather than think. This matters even on a personal level. A high level of creative ability is a better predictor than a high level of intelligence that an individual will become an entrepreneur, inventor, author, diplomat, or doctor—the very people who sustain civilizations.[10] Indeed, we will be better off putting our trust in human ingenuity and creativity* than in the policies of the political class, the predictions of statistical models, or the complaints of those who are "educated" but who cannot think for themselves.

First, we must ask ourselves, *What is worth preserving?* Many of those who ponder this question wish to return to a more basic and primitive way of life in the form of localized societies of "the Bible and the gun." But that is not a civilization. It is not even a culture. It does not even reflect the most ancient tribal societies, where we find the craftsperson (the metallurgist, weaver, etc.) and the priest, seer, or elder,

---

*We can think of Elon Musk's launching of Tesla, which produces cars that use clean energy, as well as Boyan Slat's Ocean Cleanup device for removing trash from the ocean and Jordanian architect Abeer Seikaly, who designed self-sustainable shelters for refugees.

as well as the warrior and hunter. Many such societies have been lost to us or are remembered only through occasional archaeological finds and through myths that, often, were written down centuries after they were believed or fully understood.

Others who are unhappy with our civilization see the value—or at least the high price—we place on famous works of art, for example, and contrast this with the relatively low salaries of nurses and teachers. They feel that a civilization should prize what is useful over what is artistic, beautiful, or creative, that the hospital, politics, and science are more important than the cathedral, temple, art gallery, and museum, or than philosophy, literature, or music. "All art is quite useless," remarked Oscar Wilde.[11] And yet, as Wilde knew, although art has no "use," it uplifts us and gives our lives meaning. It can even make us aware of a greatness within that is possible for us to bring out. It can transform us because it alludes to something beyond us, some kind of cosmic greatness and beauty, some kind of divinity to which our destiny is bound. That is why we remember, admire, and are inspired by the Acropolis, the frescoes of Pompei, Michelangelo's frescoes in the Sistine Chapel, the intricacy of the kimono and samurai armor alike, the woodblock prints of Hokusai, the tile work of mosques, the Roman Colosseum, the Chinese opera, Russian churches with their strange and fairy-tale-like "onion domes," and the paintings of Hans Holbein, the symbolists, the French impressionists, and even later artists. Aesthetics is the soul of a civilization.

Without the creative and the beautiful, the warrior is merely a man without chivalry, a man who has not embraced his dual nature. And as Ibn Khaldun perhaps inadvertently warns us, without the creative individual, the warrior must watch his dynasty wither and die. (And no doubt, the opposite is true.) We find ourselves at a moment in time in which everything is in flux. Everything is changing, and much, it would seem, is collapsing. Technology has brought us far, but we are at the brink. The ship is creaking and threatens to break apart or, like the *Titanic,* risks being torn apart by some unforeseen event.

In the largely forgotten sci-fi movie *The Black Hole* (1979), a scientist by the name of Dr. Hans Reinhardt has taken over an enormous spacecraft, the USS *Cygnus,* that had left Earth some years earlier and had been thought lost. Dr. Reinhardt has commandeered the *Cygnus* and stationed it at the edge of the black hole. A genius and a madman, he has turned areas of the ship into farms. But he has also transformed its crew, from human beings into unspeaking androids dressed in monklike robes with metal visors, except for one crew member, whom he has turned into a red, hovering killer android named Maximilian, with arms that open up into various weapons.

However, more important to us than either the plot or the details of androids is the ending, which is mythical, mystical, operatic, and symbolic. The *Cygnus* enters the black hole. The sky is red. We see the monklike androids file through a rugged, primordial landscape. Maximilian appears high up on a meteoric mountain. (Notably, the mountain's shape is reflective of Maximilian's head and neck, as if he has become the universe.) The gadgets on Maximilian's arms and legs are open, and against the red sky, he appears as a science fiction rendering of the multiarmed god Shiva, "the Destroyer." It is a scene of cosmic collapse. In Hindu terms, it is the end of the Kali Yuga (the final, and the darkest, of all the ages). But then a shining corridor of arches of light appears in the gloom, and an angelic-type being leads a small spacecraft and its crew (who had discovered the *Cygnus* and have now escaped Dr. Reinhardt and his ship, which, struck by meteors, threatens to be torn apart) through to the other side—into a new galaxy and a new beginning. The mix of Hindu-like and Christian-like imagery is reminiscent of the Christian Vedanta movement. But what is important to us is the idea—a mythic idea revived in modernity—that there is a passage through the collapse.

To many today, it appears that we are living in a time akin to the third stage of Ibn Khaldun's schema of dynastic decline or at the end of the Kali Yuga.* And many negative and fanatical political fantasies have been generated in response. But what is the nature of this last stage? And how do we go through it? Zygmunt Bauman has characterized our time as "liquid modernity." In it, everything is fluid, fleeting, ambiguous, changing. And indeed, we speak of "market liquidity" and "liquid assets," of being "gender fluid," of "going with the flow" and of "flow" (the state of being immersed in an activity that one performs with full attention and ease). Everything is morphing. We are in a time in which we question even solid reality. As Jean Baudrillard observes, we no longer look for novel sexual encounters but look to discover our sexual identity.[12] The desire for the tactile yet potentially transcendent experience of sex has given way to an inner questioning about sexual identity, whether we are sexual or asexual, and so on.[13] Our gender is fluid. Everything is becoming a "simulation." A landscape becomes a photograph. An event becomes a television broadcast.[14] We ourselves become our social media profile, making sure our lives are photogenic and "shareable."

"Be like water," Bruce Lee advised students of the martial arts. Water can trickle gently down a wall or it can become a tidal wave, destroying everything in its path. Water, or "liquid," has a double nature in itself and in relation to humanity. Metaphorically, it suggests high intelligence (someone who knows how to manage and maximize

---

*Hence, the proliferation of books and articles predicting "the end of the American empire," "the end of a nation," "the end of Europe," "the end of capitalism," "the death of the West," "the end of human civilization by 2050," and so on.

liquid assets, for example) and higher consciousness (flow). But in relation to human invention, water is also tied to quantity. Having been unable to measure the volume of irregular objects, the ancient Greek scientist Archimedes (c. 287–c. 212 BCE) solved the problem when he stepped into a bath. Noticing the water rise, he realized that the volume of water displaced would be equal to that of any object placed into it and thus could be used to measure irregular objects.

So in water, we have the symbolism of both elevated consciousness and pure quantity of matter. In liquid modernity, then, importance is placed on the specialist (the person of high intellect) who can manage quantity (e.g., the economist or the stock market trader). Another manifestation of this duality is the positive thinking movement in its most crass and populist form, in which individuals hope to achieve greater material wealth through mental power—or "mindset"—alone. In such an age, it is essential for us—and for the creative minority, who can shine a light through the black hole—to be able to both think and create. One of these is not enough. The vision of the future must be worked out in art, architecture, literature, agriculture, and technology— as much in the spacecraft as in the sculpture.

We have spoken of Ibn Khaldun's notion of dynasties having three stages. To gain a better understanding of where we are, we might liken these to the craftsman, warrior, and priest or magician, which were the three castes of Indo-European society as discerned by philologist Georges Dumézil (though we find these castes, vocations, or archetypes in probably every developed culture and in different guises, including in today's civilizations).* Since cultures go out of balance, each archetype

*For an overview of the myths, symbols, and ritual practices associated with these three archetypes, see my book *Three Stages of Initiatic Spirituality: Craftsman, Warrior, Magician*, Inner Traditions, 2020.

will go up or down in importance over time, sometimes characterizing a period and sometimes being made to serve the dominant caste or profession, which becomes so powerful as to become a worldview. In Ibn Khaldun's schema, the first stage is that of the warrior. The warrior conquers a dynasty and rules it. The second stage we might liken to the craftsman. There is an appreciation for culture and luxury, though there is still an appreciation for strength and stoic values. The third stage we might liken to the priest or magician. It is the stage of the intellect, of rationalizing, and of the belief that things should be perfect.

We can discern the warrior, craftsman, and priest or magician schema in history. In regard to the Roman empire, this begins with the founding of Rome by the mythological warriors Romulus and Remus (who were suckled by a she-wolf) in 753 BCE and wars of expansion, followed by a period of construction (especially from circa 380 BCE) and the building of roads, temples, theaters, and the Colosseum, and then, finally, the abandonment of the cult of the emperors and of polytheistic religion and the adoption of Christianity as the official religion of Rome (380 CE). Or, again, we might compare Ibn Khaldun's schema to the European medieval period with its crusades, followed by the Renaissance and industrial revolution, and then by the modern era.

Despite our scientific advances, there is much in our society today that is reminiscent of magic, even if much of it has emerged unconsciously. Over the last century or so, there has been a revival, or the reinvention, of pre-Christian religions (Druidry, Wicca, and other forms of neopaganism). Outside of religion, there is a widespread belief in angels and the supernatural. In business, the power of visualization and the mind, or mindset, to produce success is increasingly accepted. Outside of spirituality, there is a growing belief that our feelings should outweigh any facts that contradict them (and even scientific studies are interpreted and misinterpreted by the press, while some prominent scientists adjust or reverse their conclusions based on what the latest political issue seems to demand). Even the sexual ambiguity of modernity reflects the ancient tribal shaman, who by cross-dressing united the male and female nature in himself, thus positioning himself somewhere between the human and the gods.

The forces that guide society are generally unconscious and work through the collective and hence, through superstition, widespread fear, popular opinion, mob violence, and—in places where the populace is uneducated and does not know how to think but is only capable of absorbing opinions—through democracy itself. In many cases, around the world, nation-states have been able to retard and, to some extent, to reverse the pull of modernity by readopting and adapting their old worldview—Shia Islam in Iran, Confucianism (mixed with capitalism) in China, Hinduism (or Hindutva) in India, and Orthodox Christianity in Russia. Thus, they can hold at bay one worldview with another that is less malleable and historically and psychologically deeper rooted, even if it is opposed by a great many in these societies. Religion isn't the only weapon, however. A critic of brutalist-style modern architecture, the philosopher Roger Scruton, remarked that no one would object if cities were built in the style of the city of Bath.[15] And that, of course, is true. With roots going back all the way back to 60 BCE, Bath is almost certainly Britain's most beautiful city. But reconstructing such cities is not suitable for a country with over sixty-five million people or a world with eight billion people. We cannot endlessly replicate the past.

The only way to move through the black hole and gravitational pull of unconscious forces is to become conscious. This is the work of each individual. But it is especially important that creative individuals begin to conceive of the future aesthetically rather than politically. The religions have enabled the faithful to see through and beyond the collapse by positing the appearance of a divine being who will guide us, such as Kalki, Jesus, or the Mahdi, or the appearance of a new golden age, such as the Hindu Satya Yuga. What is needed are new ideas that take account of human nature and the natural environment and that incorporate the best of tradition with innovation. We must revive the imagination and cultivate creativity. We must become generalists, able to draw inspiration, ideas, and problem-solving techniques from different and seemingly unrelated areas of life. Only then will we evolve a new aesthetic suitable for whatever is beyond the black hole into which we find ourselves increasingly drawn. In regard to architecture, the more visionary architects of our age have begun incorporating nature into buildings, especially in Asia. This will ultimately prove a better model than Bath, which cannot be rebuilt in different locations.

Though we may live to see the black hole of a dystopian future, we must face the fact that there will never be a utopia on Earth. Wars, violence, pandemics, and economic collapse will occur. If we remain fully human, there will still be death, sickness, and heartbreak. Societies will rise and fall. But on a stormy sea, the sailor must know the direction of the land he is sailing to, even if he cannot yet see it.

13

ARISE, THE HIGHER INDIVIDUAL

WE HAVE CALLED THE CREATIVE INDIVIDUAL the Tantric priest of our society. Consider the Hindu Tantric Rite of Five *M*s, which are *madya* (wine), *māṃsa* (meat), *matsya* (fish), *mudrā* (parched grain), and *maithuna* (sexual intercourse). The practitioner of this rite consumes alcohol, meat, and other substances forbidden to him by the strict code of his society and engages in sexual intercourse with a member of a different caste, breaking another cultural taboo. From society's perspective, it is a deeply immoral act. Yet the purpose of the rite is to free the Tantric practitioner from the limits of his own thinking so that he can see the divine in things and even in people that he thought of as unclean.

This is much like our conception of the higher individual or the higher man. If society is against masculinity, he develops his masculine nature. If it is against the feminine, he develops his feminine side—his anima—through art or poetry, or through appreciating beauty, or through intellectus (contemplation). But he is not a sulky child, reflexively rebelling against society and developing one side of himself to cause shock. Indeed, upon recognizing that society or, perhaps, even civilization is in flux, drifting slowly from one worldview to another, and upon recognizing that it will sooner or later abandon the values it currently holds as absolute and unquestionable, he does not make society his measure. Rather, he looks simultaneously to the past and to the future; to the eternal, archetypal, and ancient and to possibility and vision. He looks to the heroes and creative individuals of the past for guidance and, ready for the future, develops his whole being. His emphasizing of those archetypes that society represses is a Tantric act. It is a shock to the system, but to the breaker of the taboo, it reveals that God is as present in the shadows as He is in the light.

Since World War II, in the West, in particular, the warrior and the creative individual—especially the artist—have been distinct and, generally, very much opposed, with the former representing tradition (including traditional religion), law and order, borders, patriotism, and so on, and the latter representing experimentation, revolution, open borders, and openness to other cultures. This is a rift and not an example of an archetypal duality.

Yet even if they have been very distinct and in opposition over the last half a century or more, the warrior and the creative individual have often been unified in the higher type of individual. Where this has occurred, there has often been a strong element of spiritual practice, even a spiritual awakening. Yamaoka Tesshu and Omori Sogen were both masters of calligraphy, sword fighting, and Zen Buddhism.[1] In India, the Buddha—who was born into the warrior caste—was always considered to have been an expert wrestler, though he is revered as a spiritual teacher and avatar of the god Vishnu. The feared Norse warrior Egill Skallagrímsson was also a renowned poet. The samurai warrior Miyamoto Musashi was also a calligrapher, painter, and gardener.

At the beginning of this book, we said that the warrior had a dual nature, and in this regard we mentioned C. S. Lewis's belief that chivalry placed a "double demand" on the warrior (i.e., to be both fierce and meek). He has to work to cultivate these qualities. Or if one comes naturally to him, then he must work on the other. And we have seen, too, that the higher type of warrior cultivates not only the arts of war but also the arts of peace—painting, calligraphy, poetry—as well as spirituality and philosophical insight. Authentic art involves not only some skill with the hands or the body but also the invaluable but lost practice of observing and contemplating. It is essential that the higher type of individual should practice an art as well as the arts of war (self-defense, physical training, strategy, negotiation, diplomacy, etc.).

Of course, all men are contradictory, but because most men never explore or develop themselves, they are able to mask over their own contradictions. A man likes his wife, boss, and friends one day and dislikes them the next. He sometimes daydreams about power or sex or of running away and starting again, but he goes on with his routine, which gives him little pleasure and sense of purpose. He is a lukewarm sinner and a tepid saint, and when he sins, he wishes to be a saint, and when he acts as a saint, he thinks instead of being a sinner. He does not live toward anything—toward his Higher Self—but merely resides in the middle of the churning momentum of society and is unknowingly swept along by it until, perhaps, he is overwhelmed by it.

On our ongoing and, perhaps, lifelong journey toward the Higher Self, we will inevitably find our own duality becoming more pronounced. Neither sexual desire nor petty jealousies, nor anger, nor laziness and excuse-making magically disappear just because we have begun to cultivate a higher consciousness. Yet we are not aiming to inflate our inner contradictory nature and desires but to sublimate them Though he still wrestles with the passions, the higher type of individual frees himself from inner chaos and contradiction by embodying a higher duality. Symbolized by the yin and the yang, by Bolverker and the giantess Gunnloth in Norse mythology, by the alchemical hermaphrodite Rebis, and so on, the union of opposites brings forth life and new dynamic energy.

Thus, the "opposites" within the higher type of individual become "complementaries." He is demanding of himself and forgiving of others. He is possessed by a strong vision but listens to others and wants to hear their honest opinions. He is supremely confident in his knowledge and humble enough to listen to and to learn from someone even of lesser knowledge. He cultivates the body and the intellect. He unifies the masculine and the feminine. He is a warrior and a mystic. He is fully conscious of his mortality and abundantly full of life. He respects and builds on tradition to bring new creativity—which destroys and sweeps away whatever is fossilizing—and with that, he brings new life, new energy, and new possibilities.

The process, for which we have borrowed Toynbee's term "withdrawal-and-return," can be described by the alchemical *solve et coagula*. Something is dissolved so that something of greater value can coagulate and emerge from it. In this case, it is the ego that is dissolved in order for the coagulation of a higher consciousness, the Higher Self. We have dissolved our inner critical voice to become a creator. And we have dissolved fear into faith. Likewise, we did not—and will not—join a group to submerge ourselves in it, evading self-responsibility, but rather to learn, to be held accountable to our own aspirations, and over a long period, to develop as a leader within it, to inspire others, and to pass on what we have learned. Similarly, we did not study an art to remain forever a student, but rather to become a master, letting our own style slowly emerge along with our own understanding of the art and of the world.

In America, in particular, there is often a great emphasis placed on—or a fetishizing of—one's "teacher." (Perhaps this is because people feel adrift and want to connect themselves to an authority.) And we hear spiritual practitioners of thirty or forty years declaring that we are all really "students." But at some point, we also have to accept the responsibility to become a teacher, to say not "this is what my guru thinks" but "this is what I think." Only by taking such responsibility can the higher individual show us a path out of the chaos.

On our journey, we have left the security and comfort of home. We have entered chaos, becoming conscious of the primordial and of what has sustained civilizations and cultures across time and space. As we draw this subject to a close, let's reflect on the attitude and some of the ideas and techniques that we have looked at and how you might implement these in your daily life. First, let's look at the attitude we need to cultivate.

First and foremost, you must kill your inner critic, which cannibalizes your thoughts and your creativity. Demonic in its very being, your inner critic feeds on criticism, loving the criticism it hears of others, and becoming maddened and energized by criticism of your beliefs (if we can even say that those beliefs are really yours). Do not become involved in worthless arguments with people who know they are exaggerating and lying or who lack the intelligence to really think for themselves. Do not become swept up in the hysteria of the moment. Fanatical beliefs are soon rationalized away. Hold yourself to a higher standard. See yourself as not on a particular "side" but as someone who is in search of the truth and who, like Sir Gawain, is prepared to go out into the unknown to find it. Real knowledge and understanding require us to risk being wrong, just as long-term success inevitably means experiencing some failures along the way.

As Gawain respects the Green Knight, find others of intelligence and compassion who disagree with you but have thought deeply to come to that position. Genuinely seek to understand their position and adopt what is true or noble in their beliefs, even if it is one small thing. Take what is good and reject what is bad. Do not pay much attention to critics. Plenty of people will say you cannot do something. Do they really know you? Do you even know what you are capable of? In time, the critic is forgotten. In this world, only the creator remains alive after his death.

Become a creator of an art and of your life. Turn your attention to what you can do. Do not idly fantasize. Focus on what is possible even as you work toward what seems impossible right now. Have a clear aim and move toward it, taking small but consistent steps. Practice each and every day. Wake up early if you have to and practice before other people are awake. Cut out time-wasting entertainment and activities. Turn distracting technology off. Though you should maintain close bonds with others who are of value to you, cut down on socializing if you have to, especially with acquaintances.

But more than having an aim and more than working toward it, as a creator, see the good in things. Be interested in culture and history. Find beauty where others do not. Find immortality in what is fleeting. Find profundity in simple things.

Do not be fooled by those who speak in ambiguities, using words to disguise their thoughts and intentions and, sometimes, their lack of understanding. Know your subject well enough to explain it simply. And speak simply and with conviction.

Do not give in to obstacles. See the challenges, difficulties, weaknesses, and disadvantages that you have had to face, or are facing now, as a source of strength, forcing you to focus, to look deeper, or to think differently from others and to find how your limitations can be turned to your advantage. "Good luck," such as family connections, can help people to secure lucrative careers. But they are often insecure and unhappy. Those who become masters in their field, in contrast, have very often had to wrestle with serious afflictions, illnesses, learning disabilities, abuse, or poverty at a young age. It gives them drive and an understanding of the human condition. It forces them to become creative and ingenious. And it makes them take manageable risks rather than trying to have a comfortable, easy life. As Sun Tzu says in *The Art of War*, in desperate situations soldiers lose their fear and, feeling that there is no middle ground between death and victory, they will fight hard.[2] Instead of feeling unlucky or unfortunate, see your disadvantage as your particular advantage, as what will make you fight harder and with greater skill.

Do not give up if things do not go your way at first. If a skill, art, or path is of value, it will take time—often many years. Those who experience quick and easy success often give up before everyone else. Persist, and see if your chosen path is for you. Perhaps you will need to adjust your course. Perhaps it will lead you to another avenue. Perhaps you will discover that it is not your calling after all. The time won't have been wasted. You will have developed the discipline you need to pursue another path. And as the *Hagakure* intimates, having practiced one Way, it will be easier for you to develop yourself in another. The individual who has developed the habit of contemplating, looking deeper at things than have other people, and who has developed confidence and humility will be able to adapt to new challenges and new paths. Painting, writing, philosophy, music, writing, martial arts—all of these share fundamental principles.

In contrast to modern work, which is specialized and forces us to focus on one small aspect somewhere in the middle of a process, cultivate an art or a skill that takes you through from beginning to end. Do not become a "specialist," developing only one side of yourself to please others. Defy clichés. Do not do what is expected. Learn widely and from different arts and sciences, finding connections that others cannot see.

Life isn't easy. It is hard and can be brutal. The techniques and attitude outlined in this book are intended to help you get through the toughest times and circumstances, to help you excel in more fortuitous times and circumstances, and to help you discover and become your true Self. But though we can gain ever more control over our own thoughts, emotions, and actions, we cannot choose the time in which we must live. Dynasties rise and fall. The warrior energy dissipates. Creativity wanes. Society loses direction and spins in circles. Yet you must resist its gravitational pull, its criticism, its attempts to drag down. Look to the future. Stand up as a visionary, a creator, a mystic, and a warrior. Your great work may become the seed of a new culture.

NOTES

INTRODUCTION

1. Eliade, *Shamanism,* 103.

1. THE DUAL QUALITY OF THE WARRIOR

1. Morris, *Naked Ape,* 22–24.
2. Morris, *Naked Ape,* 9.
3. Byock, *Saga of the Volsungs,* 1.
4. Byock, *Saga of the Volsungs,* 72.
5. Morris and Magnusson, *Story of the Volsungs* (Volsunga Saga).
6. Lewis, *Present Concerns,* 1–6.
7. Online Etymology Dictionary, s.v. "virile (adj.)."
8. Butler, *Charles George Gordon,* 85.
9. Conrad and Demarest, *Religion and Empire,* 28–29.
10. Ibn Khaldun, *Muqaddimah,* 136–38.
11. Internet Encyclopedia of Philosophy, s.v. "The Sophists (Ancient Greek)."
12. Hegel, *Philosophy of Right,* xix.
13. Cassirer, *Myth of the State,* 283.
14. Mishima, *Sun and Steel,* 8.
15. Mishima, *Sun and Steel,* 24.

16. Mishima, *Sun and Steel,* 19.
17. Ouspensky, *In Search of the Miraculous,* 274.
18. De Törne, *Sibelius,* 27.
19. Worcester and McComb, *Body, Mind, and Spirit,* 201–3. See also Horowitz, "Take the 30-Day Mental Challenge."
20. Aurelius, *Meditations,* IV. 12.

2. NOBLE FRIENDSHIP

1. Winny, *Sir Gawain,* 16–17.
2. MacIntyre, *After Virtue,* 124–26.
3. Winny, *Sir Gawain,* 22–23.
4. Winny, *Sir Gawain,* 24–25.
5. Sulami, *Way of Sufi Chivalry,* 37–42.
6. Putnam, *Bowling Alone,* 60. See also Hari, *Lost Connections,* 72–90.
7. Bhikkhu, "Upaddha Sutta."
8. Benjamin Franklin Historical Society, "Junto Club."
9. Horowitz, *Power of the Master Mind,* 3.
10. Horowitz, *Power of the Master Mind,* 18–20.
11. Tyson, *Iron Ambition,* 81.
12. Tyson, *Iron Ambition,* 46–51.
13. Bellows, *Poetic Edda,* 37.
14. Epictetus, *Golden Sayings of Epictetus,* 178.
15. Griffiths, *Cosmic Revelation,* 39.

3. THE NECESSARY WORK

1. Plato, *Republic,* Book III.
2. Sri Aurobindo, *Hour of God,* 21–22.
3. *Ynglinga Saga,* 7; Bellows, *Poetic Edda,* "Lokasenna," 24.
4. Fischer et al., "Ancestor Effect."
5. Camus, *Rebel,* 297.
6. Rand, *Virtue of Selfishness,* 25.

4. FROM OBSTACLE TO ACCOMPLISHMENT

1. Proverbs 27:17.
2. Gladwell, *Outliers,* 65–67.
3. Gladwell, *Outliers,* 26.
4. Gladwell, *Outliers,* 67.
5. Rosoff, "Only Reason."
6. Neely, "Axl Rose."
7. Russian, "Charlize Theron."
8. Ramsay, "Ramsay: No One Should Suffer."
9. Tank et al., "Gordon Ramsay: 'I Should Never.'"
10. Summers, "Soccer Aid."
11. Braswell, "Great Writers Who Suffered." See also Ross, *Shakespeare's Tremor and Orwell's Cough.*
12. Archer, *ADHD Advantage,* 193.
13. Dallek, "Medical Ordeals of JFK."
14. Dalton, *Theodore Roosevelt,* 35–36.
15. Cummins, *History's Great Untold Stories,* 25.
16. *Irish Daily Mail,* "From Sickness to Immortality."
17. Prideaux, *Edvard Munch,* 229.
18. Nietzsche, *Twilight of the Idols,* 2.
19. Hemingway, *Farewell to Arms,* 226.
20. Taleb, *Antifragile,* 3.
21. Society for Neuroscience, "Dyslexia."
22. Kelly, "Quarter of CEOs Are Dyslexic."
23. Harlow, "Childhood Battle with Dyslexia."
24. Elkins, "Self-Made Millionaire."
25. Gittelsohn, "Charles Schwab."
26. Cox, "Learning Disability."
27. Silberman, *NeuroTribes,* 252.
28. Chapman, "Autism a Silicon Valley Asset."
29. Brite, *Courtney Love,* 25.
30. Robertson, "Gary Numan."
31. Lindauer, *Devouring Frida,* 55.

32. Kettenmann, *Kahlo,* 17–18.

33. Basu, "Story behind David Bowie's Unusual Eyes."

34. Da Costa Jr., "Chamber of Reflection."

35. Burgan, *Nikola Tesla,* 87.

36. Cooper, *Truth about Tesla,* 25.

37. *New York Herald Tribune,* "Tesla Predicts New Source of Power."

5. THE DISCIPLINE OF POSITIVE THINKING

1. Neal, "Stress Levels Soar."

2. Freud, *Mass Psychology and Other Writings,* 71.

3. Muller, *Zend-Avesta,* 247.

4. Muller, *Dhammapada,* 7.

5. Tyson, *Iron Ambition,* 48–55, 80.

6. Horowitz, *One Simple Idea,* 147–48.

7. Peale, *Positive Imaging,* 13.

8. Peale, *Positive Imaging,* 17.

9. Horowitz, "6 Tips."

10. Divine, *8 Weeks to SEALFIT,* 211–13.

6. DEVELOPING A POWERFUL SELF-IMAGE

1. Maltz, *Psycho-Cybernetics,* xvii.

2. Rychlowska et al., "Heterogeneity of Long-History Migration."

3. Rychlowska et al., "Heterogeneity of Long-History Migration."

4. Cesare, "What Your Smile Says."

5. Wilde, *Intentions.*

6. Online Etymology Dictionary, s.v. "person (n.)."

7. Taylor, *Orwell,* 57.

8. Reich, *Function of the Orgasm,* 299.

9. Reich, *Function of the Orgasm,* 300.

10. Lambert, *Kung Fu Wu Su,* 332–33.

11. Musashi, *Complete Book of Five Rings,* 47.

12. Hopcke, *Persona,* 28–29.

13. Hopcke, *Persona*, 30.

14. Hopcke, *Persona*, 27–28.

15. Hopcke, *Persona*, 44–45.

16. Maltz, *Psycho-Cybernetics*, 3–5.

17. Maltz, *Psycho-Cybernetics*, xx.

18. Suzuki, *Introduction to Zen Buddhism*, 104.

19. Hill, *Law of Success*, 275–77.

20. Hill, *Law of Success*, 277.

21. Hill, *Law of Success*, 277.

7. FEAR AND THE HIGHER SELF

1. Furedi, *How Fear Works*, 5.

2. Bauman, *Liquid Modernity*, 81.

3. Aurelius, *Meditations of Marcus Aurelius*, IV.12.

4. Muller, *Dhammapada*, 45.

5. Sample, "Julius Caesar."

6. Online Etymology Dictionary, s.v. "truth (n.)"

7. Online Etymology Dictionary, s.v. "trust (n.)"

8. Bellows, *Poetic Edda*, "Hávamál," 139.

9. Aurelius, *Meditations of Marcus Aurelius*, 204.

10. Menkes, *Better under Pressure*, 49.

11. Vasiliev and Meredith, *Let Every Breath*, 58.

12. Morris, *Naked Ape*, 180.

13. Soho, *Unfettered Mind*, 23.

14. Trungpa, *Smile at Fear*, 16.

15. Trungpa, *Smile at Fear*, 19.

16. Menkes, *Better under Pressure*, 63.

8. VENTURING INTO THE GREAT UNKNOWN

1. Winny, *Sir Gawain*, 37.

2. Winny, *Sir Gawain*, 39.

3. Winny, *Sir Gawain*, 37.

4. Winny, *Sir Gawain,* 32–35.

5. Sarkar, *Beyond Good and Evil,* 6.

6. Chesterton, *Orthodoxy,* 16.

7. Leggett, *Zen and the Ways,* 218–19.

8. Besserman and Steger, *Zen Radicals, Rebels, and Reformers,* 166.

9. Hoffer, *True Believer,* 31.

10. Mirandola, *On the Dignity of Man,* 19.

9. THE MECHANICAL WORLD AND THE PRIMORDIAL WORLD

1. Baudrillard, *Why Hasn't Everything Already Disappeared?,* 10.

2. Daub, *Four-Handed Monsters,* 70.

3. Baudrillard, *Why Hasn't Everything Already Disappeared?,* 11.

4. Cassirer, *Language and Myth,* 5.

5. Cassirer, *Language and Myth,* 7.

6. Anxiety and Depression Association of America, "Facts & Statistics."

7. Ginsburg, *Gurdjieff Unveiled,* 38–39.

8. Fitzgerald, *Frithjof Schuon,* xx.

9. Pieper, *Divine Madness,* 48.

10. Pieper, *Divine Madness,* 44.

11. Razi, *Razi's Traditional Psychology,* 38.

12. Motala, "Tall Buildings in Makkah."

13. Catholic News Agency, "Where 'No Religion' Is Default."

14. BBC News, "Earliest Music Instruments Found."

15. Radford, "World's Oldest Jewellery."

16. Whitney, *Century Dictionary and Cyclopedia,* 495.

10. TECHNOLOGICAL NOISE AND INNER SILENCE

1. Illich, "Silence Is a Commons."

2. Jünger, *Forest Passage,* 27.

3. Jünger, *Forest Passage,* 27.

4. Bronson and Merryman, "Creativity Crisis."

5. Pieper, *Leisure,* 22.

6. Pieper, *Leisure,* 38.

7. Pieper, *Leisure,* 21.

8. Pieper, *Leisure,* 28–29.

9. Pieper, *Leisure,* 26.

11. SEX, ORGASM, AND DEATH

1. Wilson, *Age of Defeat,* 29.

2. Sulami, *Way of Sufi Chivalry,* 13–14.

3. Paglia, *Sexual Personae,* 20.

4. Frawley, *Tantric Yoga,* 114.

5. Winny, *Sir Gawain,* 60–61.

6. Winny, *Sir Gawain,* 68–75.

7. Baumeister, "Reality of the Male Sex Drive."

8. Winny, *Sir Gawain,* 78–79.

9. Winny, *Sir Gawain,* 80–93.

10. Winny, *Sir Gawain,* 66–67.

11. Winny, *Sir Gawain,* 66–67.

12. Winny, *Sir Gawain,* 82–83.

13. Winny, *Sir Gawain,* 84–85.

14. Stefani et al., "Sexual Activity before Sports Competition."

15. Razi, *Razi's Traditional Psychology,* 81.

16. Hill, *Think and Grow Rich,* 260–90.

17. Winny, *Sir Gawain,* 38–39.

18. Winny, *Sir Gawain,* 34–35.

19. Winny, *Sir Gawain,* 116–17.

20. Winny, *Sir Gawain,* 16–17.

12. THE WARRIOR AND THE CREATIVE INDIVIDUAL

1. Winny, *Sir Gawain,* 130–31.

2. Winny, *Sir Gawain,* 126–33.

3. Weiner, "Violence and Mental Illness," 175.

4. Symons, *Art of Aubrey Beardsley,* 37.

5. Toynbee, *Study of History,* 241.

6. Toynbee, *Study of History,* 213.

7. Toynbee, *Study of History,* 214–15.

8. Toynbee, *Study of History,* 216.

9. Sarkar, *Beyond Good and Evil,* 47.

10. Bronson and Merryman, "Creativity Crisis."

11. Wilde, "Picture of Dorian Gray."

12. Baudrillard, *America,* 48.

13. Baudrillard, *America,* 48.

14. Baudrillard, *America,* 32.

15. *Spectator* website, "Full Transcript: Douglas Murray in Conversation with Roger Scruton."

13. ARISE, THE HIGHER INDIVIDUAL

1. Sogen, *Introduction to Zen Training,* xiii.

2. Sun Tzu, *Art of War,* 94.

BIBLIOGRAPHY

Anxiety and Depression Association of America. "Facts & Statistics." Accessed July 5, 2020.

Archer, Dale. *The ADHD Advantage: What You Thought Was a Diagnosis May Be Your Greatest Strength.* New York: Avery, 2015.

Aurelius, Marcus. *The Meditations of Marcus Aurelius.* Translated by George Long. New York: P. F. Collier & Son Corporation, 1937.

Basu, Tanya. "The Story behind David Bowie's Unusual Eyes." *The Cut,* January 12, 2016.

Baudrillard, Jean. *America.* Translated by Verso. London: Verso, 2010.

———. *Why Hasn't Everything Already Disappeared?* Translated by Chris Turner. London: Seagull Books, 2016.

Bauman, Zygmunt. *Liquid Modernity.* Cambridge: Polity, 2000.

Baumeister, Roy F. "The Reality of the Male Sex Drive." *Psychology Today,* December 8, 2010.

BBC News. "Earliest Music Instruments Found." May 25, 2012.

Bellows, Henry Adams, trans. *The Poetic Edda: The Mythological Poems.* Mineola, N.Y.: Dover Publications, Inc.

Benjamin Franklin Historical Society. "Junto Club." Accessed July 4, 2020.

Besserman, Perle, and Manfred B. Steger. *Zen Radicals, Rebels, and Reformers.* Boston: Wisdom Publications, 2011.

Bhikkhu, Thanissaro, trans. "Upaddha Sutta: Half of the Holy Life." Buddha Sutra website. Accessed July 4, 2020.

Braswell, Sean. "The Great Writers Who Suffered Greatly from Physical Ailments." Ozy website. Accessed July 4, 2020.

Brite, Poppy Z. *Courtney Love: The Real Story.* New York: A Touchstone Book, Simon & Schuster, 1997.

Bronson, Po, and Ashley Merryman. "The Creativity Crisis." *Newsweek,* July 10, 2010.

Burgan, Michael. *Nikola Tesla: Physicist, Inventor, Electrical Engineer.* Minneapolis: Compass Point Books, 2009.

Butler, Sir William Francis. *Charles George Gordon.* London: MacMillan and Co., 1889.

Byock, Jesse L., trans. *The Saga of the Volsungs: The Norse Epic of Sigurd the Dragon Slayer.* London: Penguin Books, 1999.

Camus, Albert. *The Rebel: An Essay on Man in Revolt.* Translated by Anthony Bower. New York: Vintage International, 1991.

Cassirer, Ernst. *Language and Myth.* Translated by Susanne K. Langer. New York: Dover Publications Inc., 1953.

———. *The Myth of the State.* New Haven, Conn.: Yale University Press, 1974.

Catholic News Agency. "Where 'No Religion' Is Default, A Look at Europe's Young Catholic Minority." March 22, 2018.

Cesare, Chris. "What Your Smile Says about Where You're From." *Science,* May 5, 2015.

Chapman, Glenn. "Autism a Silicon Valley Asset with Social Quirks." Phys.org. August 28, 2016.

Chesterton, G. K. *Orthodoxy.* New York: John Lane Company, 1908.

Conrad, Geoffrey W., and Arthur A. Demarest. *Religion and Empire: The Dynamics of Aztec and Inca Expansionism.* Cambridge: Cambridge University Press, 1984.

Cooper, Christopher. *The Truth about Tesla: The Myth of the Lone Genius in the History of Innovation.* New York: Race Point Publishing, 2015.

Cox, David. "A Learning Disability Often Makes for a More Visionary, Innovative CEO." Quartz website. May 29, 2015.

Cummins, Joseph. *History's Great Untold Stories: Larger than Life Characters and Dramatic Events That Changed the World.* Washington, D.C.: National Geographic, 2007.

Da Costa, Helio L., Jr. "The Chamber of Reflection." Masonic Trowel. October 16, 1999.

Dallek, Robert. "The Medical Ordeals of JFK." *The Atlantic,* December 2002.

Dalton, Kathleen. *Theodore Roosevelt: A Strenuous Life.* New York: Vintage Books, 2004.

Daub, Adrian. *Four-Handed Monsters: Four-Hand Piano Playing and Nineteenth-Century Culture.* Oxford: Oxford University Press, 2014.

De Törne, Bengt: *Sibelius: A Close-Up.* Boston: Houghton Mifflin Company, 1938.

Divine, Mark. *8 Weeks to SEALFIT.* New York: St. Martin's Griffin, 2014.

Eliade, Mircea. *Shamanism: Archaic Techniques of Ecstasy.* Translated by Willard R. Trask. Bollingen Series LXXVI. Princeton, N.J.: Princeton University Press, 2004.

Elkins, Kathleen. "A Self-Made Millionaire Who Studied 1,200 Wealthy People Found They All Have One—Free—Pastime in Common." *Business Insider* website. August 21, 2015.

Epictetus. *The Golden Sayings of Epictetus.* Translated by Hastings Crossley. Edited by Charles W. Eliot. New York: Collier & Son Corporation, 1937.

Fischer, Peter, Anne Sauer, Claudia Vogrincic, and Silke Weisweiler. "The Ancestor Effect: Thinking about Our Genetic Origin Enhances Intellectual Performance." *European Journal of Social Psychology* 41, no. 1 (February 2011): 11–16.

Fitzgerald, Michael Oren. *Frithjof Schuon: Messenger of the Perennial Philosophy.* Bloomington, Ind.: World Wisdom, 2010.

Frawley, David. *Tantric Yoga and the Wisdom Goddesses.* Twin Lakes, Wis.: Lotus Press, 2003.

Freud, Sigmund. *Mass Psychology and Other Writings.* Translated by J. A. Underwood. London: Penguin Books, 2004.

Furedi, Frank. *How Fear Works.* London: Bloomsbury Continuum, 2018.

Ginsburg, Seymour B. *Gurdjieff Unveiled: An Overview and Introduction to the Teaching.* Great Britain: Lighthouse Workbooks, 2005.

Gittelsohn, John. "Charles Schwab Has a $3.6 Trillion Edge on the Fintechs: The 81-Year-Old Discount-Investing Pioneer Is Taking on a New Crop of Rivals." Bloomberg. October 2, 2018.

Gladwell, Malcolm. *Outliers: The Story of Success*. New York: Little, Brown and Company, 2008.

Griffiths, Bede. *The Cosmic Revelation: The Hindu Way to God*. Springfield, Ill.: Templegate Publishers, 1983.

Hari, Johann. *Lost Connections: Uncovering the Real Causes of Depression—And the Unexpected Solutions*. New York: Bloomsbury, 2018.

Harlow, Poppy. "Childhood Battle with Dyslexia Brings Shark Tank's 'Mr. Wonderful' to Tears." CNN Business. April 1, 2016.

Hegel, G. W. F. *Philosophy of Right*. Translated by S. W. Dyde. Mineola, N.Y.: Dover Publications, Inc., 2005.

Hemingway, Ernest. *A Farewell to Arms*. New York: Scribner, 1997.

Hill, Napoleon. *The Law of Success*. New York: Jeremy P. Tarcher/Penguin, 2008.

———. *Think and Grow Rich*. Meriden, Conn.: The Ralston Society, 2017.

Hoffer, Eric. *The True Believer: Thoughts on the Nature of Mass Movements*. New York: Harper Perennial, 1951.

Hopcke, Robert H. *Persona: Where Sacred Meets Profane*. Boston: Shambhala, 1995.

Horowitz, Mitch. *One Simple Idea: How the Lessons of Positive Thinking Can Transform Your Life*. New York: Crown Publishers, 2014.

———. *The Power of the Master Mind*. United States of America: Gildan Media LLC, the Napoleon Hill Foundation, 2019.

———. "6 Tips to Visualize Your Dreams Coming True." *Guideposts* website. Accessed July 5, 2020.

———. "Take the 30-Day Mental Challenge." Science of Mind website. November 2015.

Ibn Khaldun. *The Muqaddimah: An Introduction to History*. Abridged and edited by N. J. Dawood. Translated by Franz Rosenthal. Bollingen Series. Princeton, N.J.: Princeton University Press, 2005.

Illich, Ivan. "Silence Is a Commons." *CoEvolution Quarterly*, no. 40, Winter 1983.

Internet Encyclopedia of Philosophy, s.v. The Sophists (Ancient Greek)."

Irish Daily Mail. "From Sickness to Immortality." December 28, 2018.

Jünger, Ernst. *The Forest Passage*. Translated by Thomas Friese. Edited with an introduction by Russell A. Berman. Candor, N.Y.: Telos Press Publishing, 2013.

Kelly, Ross. "A Quarter of CEOs Are Dyslexic, Says Cisco's John Chambers." Chief Executive website. March 22, 2017.

Kettenmann, Andrea. *Kahlo*. Hohenzollernring, Köln, Germany: Taschen GmbH, 1999.

Lambert, Don. *Kung Fu Wu Su: A Memoir*. United States of America: Privately printed, 2017.

Leggett, Trevor. *Zen and the Ways*. Rutland, Vt.: Charles E. Tuttle Company, 1987.

Lewis, C. S. *Present Concerns: Journalistic Essays*. New York: HarperOne, 1986. First published as "Notes on the Way." *Time and Tide* XXI (August 17, 1940): 841.

Lindauer, Margaret A. *Devouring Frida: The Art History and Popular Celebrity of Frida Kahlo*. Middletown, Conn.: Wesleyan University Press, 1999.

MacIntyre, Alasdair. *After Virtue: A Study in Moral Theory*. Notre Dame, Ind.: University of Notre Dame Press, 1984.

Maltz, Maxwell. *Psycho-Cybernetics: A New Way to Get More Living Out of Life*. Hollywood, Calif.: Wilshire Book Company, 1971.

Menkes, Justin. *Better under Pressure: How Great Leaders Bring Out the Best in Themselves and Others*. Boston: Harvard Business Review Press, 2011.

Mirandola, Pico della. *On the Dignity of Man*. Translation by Charles Glenn Wallis, Paul J. W. Miller, and Douglas Carmichael. Indianapolis: Hackett Publishing Company Inc., 1998.

Mishima, Yukio. *Sun and Steel*. Translated by John Bester. Tokyo: Kodansha International Ltd., 1970.

Mookerjie, Ajit, and Madhu Khanna. *The Tantric Way: Art, Science, Ritual*. London: Thames & Hudson, 1977.

Morris, Desmond. *The Naked Ape: A Zoologist's Study of the Human Animal*. New York: A Delta Book, 1967.

Morris, William, and Eirikr Magnusson, trans. *The Story of the Volsungs* (Volsunga Saga). London: Walter Scott Press, 1888. Available on the Project Gutenberg website.

Motala, Moulana Suhail. "Tall Buildings in Makkah; Sign of Qiyamah." Hadith Answers: An Online Source for Hadith Fatwas. Accessed July 5, 2020.

Muller, Friedrich Max, ed. *The Dhammapada: The Essential Teaching of the Buddha*. London: Watkins, 2016.

Muller, Max, ed. *The Zend-Avesta*. The Sacred Books of the East, Volume 31. Delhi: Motilal Banarsidass Publishers, 1887.

Musashi, Miyamoto. *The Complete Book of Five Rings*. Translated by Kenji Tokitsu. Boston: Shambhala Publications, Inc., 2010.

Neal, Meghan. "Stress Levels Soar in America by up to 30% in 30 Years." *New York Daily News*. June 16, 2012.

Neely, Kim. "Axl Rose: The Rolling Stone Interview." *Rolling Stone*. April 2, 1992.

New York Herald Tribune. "Tesla Predicts New Source of Power in Year." Tesla Universe Website. July 9, 1933.

Nietzsche, Friedrich. *The Twilight of the Idols*. Translated by Anthony M. Ludovici. Edinburgh: T. N. Foulis, 1911.

Online Etymology Dictionary, s.v. "person (n.)."

Online Etymology Dictionary, s.v. "trust (n.)."

Online Etymology Dictionary, s.v. "truth (n.)."

Online Etymology Dictionary, s.v. "virile (adj.)."

Ouspensky, P. D. *In Search of the Miraculous: Fragments of an Unknown Teaching*. San Diego: A Harvest Book, Harcourt, 2001.

Paglia, Camille. *Sexual Personae: Art and Decadence from Nefertiti to Emily Dickinson*. New York: Vintage Books, 1991.

Peale, Norman Vincent. *Positive Imaging: The Powerful Way to Change Your Life*. New York: The Random House Publishing Group, 1983.

Pieper, Josef. *Divine Madness: Plato's Case against Secular Humanism*. Translated by Lothar Krauth. San Francisco: Ignatius Press, 1995.

———. *Leisure: The Basis of Culture*. Translated by Alexander Dru. San Francisco: Ignatius Press, 1963.

Plato, *The Republic*. Book III. Translated by Benjamin Jowett. The Internet Classics Archive.

Prideaux, Sue. *Edvard Munch: Behind the Scream*. New Haven, Conn.: Yale University Press, 2005.

Putnam, Robert D. *Bowling Alone: The Collapse and Revival of American Community*. New York: Simon & Schuster Paperbacks, 2000.

Radford, Tim. "World's Oldest Jewellery Found in Cave." *Guardian,* April 16, 2004.

Ramsay, Gordon. "Ramsay: No One Should Suffer Abuse Like My Mum." CNN website. Accessed July 4, 2020.

Rand, Ayn. *The Virtue of Selfishness: A New Concept of Egoism.* New York: A Signet Book, 1964.

Razi, Abu Bakr Muḥammad ibn Zakariya' al-. *Razi's Traditional Psychology.* Translated by A. J. Arberry. Damascus: Islamic Book Service.

Reich, Wilhelm. *The Function of the Orgasm.* Translated by Vincent R. Carfagno. New York: Farrar, Straus and Giroux, 1973.

Robertson, Peter. "Gary Numan: I Don't See My Asperger's as a Disability—It's an Advantage." *Express* website. September 5, 2017.

Rosoff, Matt. "The Only Reason the Mac Looks Like It Does Is Because Steve Jobs Dropped In on a Course Taught by This Former Monk. *Business Insider,* March 8, 2016.

Ross, John J. *Shakespeare's Tremor and Orwell's Cough: The Medical Lives of Famous Writers.* New York: St. Martin's Press, 2012.

Russian, Ale. "Charlize Theron Says Her Mom, Who Shot Her Dad in Self-Defense, 'Made Me Brave.'" *People* magazine. October 16, 2018.

Rychlowska, Magdalena, Yuri Miyamoto, David Matsumoto, Ursula Hess, Eva Gilboa-Schechtman, Shanmukh Kamble, Hamdi Muluk, Takahiko Masuda, and Paula Marie Niedenthal. "Heterogeneity of Long-History Migration Explains Cultural Differences in Reports of Emotional Expressivity and the Functions of Smiles." *PNAS* 112, no. 19 (May 12, 2015): E2429–E2436.

Sample, Ian. "Julius Caesar May Have Suffered Mini-strokes, Say Doctors." *Guardian.* April 14, 2015.

Sarkar, Ranajit. *Beyond Good and Evil (A Comparative Study of the Moral Philosophies of Nietzsche and Sri Aurobindo).* Pondicherry, India: Sri Aurobindo International Centre of Education, 2002.

Silberman, Steve. *NeuroTribes: The Legacy of Autism and the Future of Neurodiversity.* New York: Avery, 2015.

Society for Neuroscience. "Dyslexia: What Brain Research Reveals about Reading." LD Online. 2004.

Sogen, Omori. *An Introduction To Zen Training: A Translation of Sanzen Nyumon.* Translated by Dogen Hosokawa and Roy Yoshimoto. Introduction by Trevor Leggett. Tokyo: Tuttle Publishing, 2001.

Soho, Takuan. *The Unfettered Mind: Writings from a Zen Master to a Master Swordsman.* Translated by William Scott Wilson. Boulder: Shambhala, 2012.

Spectator website. "Full Transcript: Douglas Murray in Conversation with Roger Scruton." May 7, 2019.

Sri Aurobindo. *The Hour of God.* Pondicherry, India: Sri Aurobindo Ashram, 1982.

Stefani, Laura, Giorgio Galanti, Johnny Padulo, Nicola L. Bragazzi, and Nicola Maffulli. "Sexual Activity before Sports Competition: A Systematic Review." *Frontiers in Psychology* 7 (June 21, 2016): 246.

Sulami, Ibn al-Husayn al-. *The Way of Sufi Chivalry.* Interpreted by Tosun Bayrak al-Jerrahi. Rochester, Vt.: Inner Traditions International, 1991.

Summers, Helen. "Soccer Aid: Did Gordon Ramsay Ever Play for Rangers, and Why Did Soccer Aid Star and Top Chef's Football Career End?" *Sun* website. June 16, 2019.

Sun Tzu. *The Art of War.* Translated by Stephen F. Kaufman. Tokyo: Tuttle Publishing, 1996.

Suzuki, Daisetz Teitaro. *An Introduction to Zen Buddhism.* New York: Grove Press, 1964.

Symons, Arthur. *The Art of Aubrey Beardsley.* Maidstone, Kent, England: Crescent Moon Publishing, 2018.

Taleb, Nassim Nicholas. *Antifragile: Things That Gain from Disorder.* New York: Random House, 2012.

Tank, Manisha, Michala Sabnani, Sol Han, and Jenni Marsh. "Gordon Ramsay: 'I Should Never Have Made It.'" CNN World. March 4, 2016.

Taylor, D. J. *Orwell: The Life.* New York: Henry Holt and Company, 2003.

Toynbee, Arnold J. *A Study of History: Abridgment of Volumes I–VI.* Abridgment by D. C. Somervell. New York: Oxford University Press, 1987.

Trungpa, Chögyam. *Smile at Fear: Awakening the True Heart of Bravery.* Boulder: Shambhala Publications, Inc., 2010.

Tyson, Mike, and Larry "Ratso" Sloman. *Iron Ambition: My Life with Cus D'Amato.* New York: Blue Rider Press, 2017.

Vasiliev, Vladimir, and Scott Meredith. *Let Every Breath: Secrets of the Russian Breath Masters*. Based on the teachings of Mikhail Ryabko. Toronto: Russian Martial Art School, Systema Headquarters, 2006.

Weiner, Jerry M. "Violence and Mental Illness in Adolescence." In *Disruptive Behavior Disorders in Children and Adolescents,* edited by Robert L. Hendren, 175–90. Washington, D.C.: American Psychiatric Press, Inc., 1999.

Whitney, William Dwight. *The Century Dictionary and Cyclopedia*. Vol. I. New York: The Century Co., 1904.

Wilde, Oscar. *Intentions*. London: Methuen & Co., Ltd., 1913. Available from the Gutenberg Project website. Accessed July 5, 2020.

———. "A Picture of Dorian Gray." *Lippincott's Monthly Magazine,* July, 1890.

Wilson, Colin. *The Age of Defeat*. London: Aristeia Press, 2018.

Winny, James, ed. and trans. *Sir Gawain and the Green Knight*. Ontario: Broadview Press, 1995.

Worcester, Elwood, and Samuel McComb. *Body, Mind, and Spirit*. New York: Charles Scribner's Sons, 1932.

The Ynglinga Saga, or the Story of the Yngling Family from Odin to Halfdan the Black. Available on the Sacred Texts website. Accessed July 4, 2020.

ABOUT THE AUTHOR

 Described by PEN Award–winning historian Mitch Horowitz as one of "a golden handful of writers who authentically and practically bridge the gap between primeval wisdom and modern spirituality," Angel Millar also bridges the gap between the warrior and the creative individual.

Living life with uncompromising intensity, Angel began studying ancient and modern spiritual traditions, and practicing various meditational and self-hypnotic techniques, in his early manhood. This led him to connect with the neopagan and esoteric world of Great Britain, and, at nineteen, he was initiated into the Illuminates of Thanateros in London, completing the mind-control curriculum for members of the order before joining.

However, rejecting much of what he encountered, in his early twenties, Angel began studying Zen Buddhism, Nam Pai Chuan Shaolin kung fu, and fine art (training at Chelsea College of Art and Design and Central Saint Martins College of Art and Design). At the same time, he also began staying annually in a Benedictine monastery in the English countryside.

Angel later moved to New York, where he has continued to develop his martial arts and meditational and positive mind practices in parallel with his philosophy of spirituality.

Today, publicly, Angel is well known as a speaker on complete self-development, spirituality, and symbolism and as the author of *The Three Stages of Initiatic Spirituality: Craftsman, Warrior, Magician,* among other books. His writing has been described by *New Dawn* magazine as "of extraordinary importance in this time of cultural and even spiritual conflict."

Privately, having developed his own system of self-development based on the archetypes of the craftsman, warrior, and magician, he mentors individuals on their own self-development journeys and provides confidential coaching, positive mind training, and hypnosis to those who are ready to take their life to the next level.

You can find out more about his public speaking as well as his coaching, positive mind training, and hypnosis at his website, angelmillar.com.

INDEX